The Engines Were Rolls Royce

THE
ENGINES WERE

AN INFORMAL HISTORY OF

ROLLS-ROYCE

THAT FAMOUS COMPANY

Ronald W. Harker

MACMILLAN PUBLISHING CO., INC.
New York

COLLIER MACMILLAN PUBLISHERS
London

Macmillan Publishing Co., Inc.
866 Third Avenue, New York, N.Y. 10022
Collier Macmillan Canada, Ltd.

Library of Congress Cataloging in Publication Data

Harker, Ronald W
    The engines were Rolls-Royce.

    1. Rolls—Royce Motors Ltd.—History.
I. Title.
HD9710.G74R563   338.7'62'9040941   79–10751
ISBN 0–02–548190–8

First Printing 1979

Printed in the United States of America

Dedication

To my mother and father,
my wife and family,
and those special people
I have had the privilege to know

Contents

Contents

Acknowledgments

I should like to thank the following, who aided me in putting this book together: my wife, Rolls-Royce Limited, Rolls-Royce Motors Ltd., Alexander Ogston, who was a great help in verifying historical and technical facts and preparing this material for publication, Sir Stanley Hooker, Sir George Edwards, Air Commodore F. R. Banks, Captain George Eyston, Air Chief Marshal Sir Neil Wheeler, Royal Aeronautical Society, Joyce Jack, Kenneth MacKenzie and Christopher Benson. Unless otherwise noted, all photographs appear courtesy of Rolls-Royce Ltd. The author gratefully acknowledges their cooperation in providing these photographs.

Foreword

BY Sir STANLEY HOOKER

C.B.E., F.R.S., D. Sc., B.Sc., D.I.C., D. Phil., F.I. Mech.E., A.R.C.Sc., Hon. F.R.Ae.S., Technical Director, Rolls-Royce (1971) Ltd., Bristol Engine Division, 1968

To me, the thrill of this book is the vivid way in which it brings back the memory of those anxious, frightening but exciting days of 1940–41, when the fate of Great Britain and its empire stood in the greatest danger.

I remember so well attending Hives's ("Hs") first technical meeting on the Monday afternoon following the declaration of war on the preceding Sunday (September 13, 1939). His opening remark was "We must win this war—it will be no use coming a good second!"

Amongst us, he was the one man who knew the responsibility which was to lie on Rolls-Royce, because he had been through it all before in World War I when the Eagle, Falcon, and Hawk engines were dominant in the air war.

Over the weekend, the Design and Technical staffs had been rapidly evacuated to accommodation in Belper—some twelve miles north of Derby. We all expected the Derby works to be bombed flat immediately, and without doubt at that time Germany had the means to do so. But Hitler made his first crucial mistake and did not act, and in consequence Derby remained in full production of the Merlin engine throughout the war.

Every Spitfire and Hurricane that fought in the Battle of Britain during the summer of 1940 was powered by Merlins made at Derby, because the great factory at Crewe was not ready for production and the factory at Glasgow was only a proposal on paper.

The Ford Motor Company, which made so many Merlin engines in later years and played such a major part in satisfying the ever growing needs for Merlins for the bombers and fighters for the RAF, had yet not begun its work. It was left to the men at Derby to toil eighteen hours a day, seven days a week to produce the Merlins for the Spitfires and Hurricanes that decisively defeated the Luftwaffe in the summer of 1940. These threw the methodical plan of the Germans—first to defeat the RAF and then to invade by sea and air—out of gear and caused the invasion to be cancelled.

At the center of this situation in Rolls-Royce sat Hs, Churchillian in physique, mentality and powers of leadership. He was the "Godfather" of us all—from shopworker to top engineer, all knew him, and saw him as he made his frequent tours of the shops to examine personally any "bottlenecks." The engineers knew him from Monday afternoon meetings where they were called to account, and by his personal inquisition during the week whenever his time permitted. Sharp in his criticism and to the point, he would immediately offer help. "I don't know how you can sleep in your beds while this state of affairs exists. What's stopping you?"—was a favorite gambit. Excuses that someone else was holding you up were answered by his picking up the telephone on the spot and sending for the one concerned. One had to be very sure of one's ground before complaining to Hs! Although the pressure he exerted was relentless, he could calm ruffled tempers and restore equanimity in an instant with a twinkle in his eye and the right quip at the right moment.

Great Britain can count its blessings that he was there as the undisputed king of Rolls-Royce at the critical hour of need of the English-speaking nations.

This book contains the personal experiences of the author, who for many years was the liaison officer between the Royal Air Force and other air forces, and the engineers of Rolls-Royce. An expert pilot himself, he was able to interpret into engineering terms the advantages, disadvantages, requirements and shortcomings of Rolls-Royce engines in actual operation. He played a very important role in telling us in just which area we needed to improve power output in order to "soup up" the Spitfire or Hurricane to beat the opposition.

This book spans a large time period but, naturally, concentrates on the postwar era when Ronnie Harker's impact on the policy and engineering thought at Rolls-Royce was at its greatest. It describes many of his efforts and interventions, and since it is written from the Rolls-Royce point of view, it obviously touches on many controversial issues.

Harker's history of the battle for the vertical takeoff aircraft is a case in point. Griffiths, at Rolls-Royce, had followed the Jules Verne idea of the multilift engine aircraft (except that Jules Verne used little propellers and not jet engines), and all that the Rolls-Royce proposal did was to muddy the waters and confuse the issues about the Harrier and the P-1154. The Harrier has since gone on to show, in operation with the RAF and the US Marine Corps, that the most practical way of achieving VTOL aircraft is with the vectored thrust single-engine configuration of the Pegasus. The multilift engine concept of Rolls-Royce was never a practical proposition for a single-seater strike fighter aircraft.

We, at the Bristol Aeroplane Company, who were on the other side of the fence, naturally have a somewhat different view of the "whys" and the "hows" and "who dun its" particularly in the late 50s and early 60s eras when Bristol was beginning to challenge Rolls-Royce's supremacy in the British aero engine field. Ronnie puts this down to the government's desire to keep a balance between the two companies, and suggests that Bristol was selected for the military projects and Rolls-Royce for the civil ones in order to maintain the balance and keep a competitive firm in operation. It may, of course, have been due to the fact that Bristol had the better engines at that period!

The internecine war which took place during this period between the two companies did neither any good and was a major contributor to indecision and the cancellation of various projects in the early 60s. Fortunately, the merger which took place in 1965 ended this, to the great advantage of the British aero engine industry.

But there is no gainsaying Harker's own personal impact on the policy and engineering concepts of Rolls-Royce, to which he gave so many years of energetic and constructive service. The RAF would be the first to acknowledge this.

Introduction

THE name of Rolls-Royce stands not only for excellence but also for honest endeavor, fair trading and good behavior. It is a name to conjure with and one for future generations to revere and emulate.

The astonishing success of the Rolls-Royce company was achieved in a very short time. To account for this, we have only to reflect upon the happy combination of the people involved: it all actually began in 1904, through the self-energized efforts of an unknown engineering genius, Henry Royce, who was introduced to an enthusiastic sporting entrepreneur, the Hon. C. S. Rolls—both of whom were managed by an exceptional businessman, Claude Johnson. The rapid rise to eminence of the Silver Ghost motor car, followed by the most successful aero engines during the first and second World Wars, was nothing short of phenomenal.

During the formative pre–World War I period, Ernest Hives began to make his mark, and he was to blossom forth into the leadership of the next generation. Ultimately, he became one of the best-known and best-liked personalities in the British engineering industry. He led the team through the most crucial and magnificent period of World War II, of which it can honestly be said: the war could have been lost but for Rolls-Royce.

The author, having had experience working in the Rolls-Royce company from 1925 up to the bankruptcy in 1971, has endeavored to portray the general outline of the company and explain the philosophy that guided it. He has further endeavored to bring out the *spirit*, the *essence*, the silver thread that throughout those years inspired the whole team of staff and workers on the shop floor to maintain the standard of excellence set by Royce and nurtured by Hives and his protégés. This standard is something that the nationalized aero engine company would do well to perpetuate; it already has taken root in Rolls-Royce Motors, the company separated from the original following the 1971 upheaval.

As one of several distinguished contributors whom I approached to help me present a well-rounded view of the original Rolls-Royce company, Air Commodore F. R. Banks, C.B.,O.B.E., kindly agreed to write a few lines on his impressions of the company. In his long and distinguished career, Rod Banks has been known throughout the world as one of the greatest authorities on internal combustion engines. (His autobiography, *I Kept No Diary*, was recently published in England.) Among his many appointments he served as a director of Bristol-Siddeley engines, managing director of the De Havilland division of Hawker-Siddeley Aviation and previous to this worked with Lord Beaverbrook at the ministry during and after the war as director general of engine development. He was recently president of the Royal Aeronautical Society.

From his knowledge of and long association with Rolls-Royce, Banks has written:

Rolls-Royce is a unique and exceptional firm, and when one looks into its history the reasons for this can be appreciated. It was started by a great engineer, Henry Royce, great because he was a meticulous mechanical engineer and impeccable detail designer. The firm itself was formed by an inspired genius, Claude Johnson, who got Royce and the Hon. C. S. Rolls together and thus created a short-lived partnership; short-lived by the death of Rolls in an aeroplane accident in 1910, but long-lived because its dedication to engineering of quality. Claude Johnson was managing director of Rolls for some years.

The 1914–18 War brought the company into the aero engine field, where it had success with the Hawk, Falcon and Eagle engines. Between wars, when the aircraft industry was gaining strength and background, Rolls-Royce remained in the aero engine business, despite the fact that the motor car was considered for some time their prime occupation.

Since Rolls did his design work away from Derby and was in poor health, it remained for the works to be particularly effective in the development of the motor car and aero engine and despite the fact that Hives, or Hs as he was called in the firm, was a manager for quite some years before he became a director, it was he who was responsible for its engineering success and who literally taught the aero engine industry what was meant by the word *development*. It really seemed to those outside that the firm's directors were largely guided by what Hives said and did; hence the individual character that has remained to this day.

I first met Hives in 1927. As an outsider I probably worked as closely, or perhaps more so, with him and his department as most other engineering representatives did and, of course, very closely in World War II and afterwards until he retired. From our contacts, over the many years I visited Rolls-Royce I saw that Hives was a great man and unlike some great men I have been privileged to meet and know, he was not petty minded.

He was no technologist and knew little of engine design or higher mathematics. Like myself, he was trained as a fitter and mechanic but he had God's gift of intuitively evaluating engine problems with a kind of sixth sense. This showed particularly in the Schneider Trophy Contest periods of 1929–31, but very markedly during the Second World War. He was in the war 100 percent and how he stood it without any real time off I don't know; but Sunday afternoons were sacrosanct, set aside only for his family. Suffice to say that in the days of the Beaver, 1940–45, (Lord Beaverbrook, minister of aircraft production), Hives was often in London, sometimes more than once a week; and once every week, while the large Glasgow plant was being built at Hillington, he spent a day and night there pretty well throughout the war. I used to see him and we often enjoyed a meal together in the canteen. One morning later at Hillington, Hives said of the work people, "Rod, they've got their strike uniform on, we won't see them back after lunch." I said, "What's the uniform, Hs, I don't see it?" He replied, "They've got their Sunday suits on under their overalls!"

Hives and his capable helpers created a hammer and chisel (Glasgow wrench) crowd into a fairly well-disciplined work force, capable of turning out quality machinery; but Hs was mainly responsible for the organization and peace-keeping. Hives was also farsighted; he came to Beaverbrook in the autumn of 1940 to suggest more power for the Spitfire, so as to be ready for the next "shooting season," meaning the "hotting-up" of air fighting in the spring of 1941. This resulted in the Spitfire V with the Merlin 45, which gave the RAF a competitive aircraft.

In retrospect, of course, one could have foreseen that Hives was going to the top. He and a friend came from Reading to find work in Derby; once in Rolls, Hives showed that he was a very competent mechanic; he also became a first-class car driver, so much so that he was included in the very social select team of Silver Ghost drivers chosen for the prewar (1914–18 War) Austrian Alpine Trials. He later drove a car at Brooklands completing the one hundred miles in an hour. Yes, "Hs" was truly great.

Lord Hives, as the chief through many critical years, was considered the personification of Rolls-Royce. He had a wonderful family to which he was devoted; then came Rolls-Royce and "work." He used to say, "There is no fun like work"; and on occasion when things were difficult he would say, "Work till it hurts." His leadership was of rare quality and came naturally, helped perhaps by his sense of humor and humanity. Claude Birch, one of his assistants who later rose to the control of a company as large as Rolls-Royce and of great renown, wrote, "I have had the privilege of working for four people in my life who I would class as great men; of all these the 'Berkshire Mechanic' towers above the rest."

Hives had a natural modesty and flare for hitting the nail on the head. He was once asked by the head of a large airline company, "To what do you attribute the success of Rolls-Royce?" Hs answered, "Maybe we are a bit better than some other people at putting our mistakes right." Another of his sage remarks was: "It is no good being right at the wrong time; the timing of a decision is paramount."

I remember going to Hs several months after the Merlin Mustang had been accepted and asking for a raise in pay. He asked me why I should have it! I replied I thought I deserved it as I was rather proud of having initiated the Merlin Mustang project. He said, "Good heavens, that's what we pay you for!" A month later, however, I was awarded another fifty pounds a year! Another of his classic sayings, when some problem was difficult to solve, was: "Ninety-nine percent of our troubles are due to something bloody silly"; this was very true.

Hives refused a knighthood during the Second World War, but accepted the Companion of Honour, an award which was a rare distinction for an engineer. Finally, in 1950, he achieved a baronetcy, the accolade he so rightly deserved: in 1946 he was made chief executive and chairman of the company, which was now greatly expanded. Some eighty thousand people were employed when Hives retired in 1957. He was elevated to the peerage and became Lord Hives of Duffield; he died in 1964, several years after suffering a stroke which made him an invalid.

The Rolls-Royce company has been unique both in its contributions to engineering and technology and in its general attitude to a changing panorama of social development, accelerated by two world wars. In order to keep and enhance its reputation of producing the "best," the management at all times encouraged the skill and sense of purpose necessary to do this. The management's dedication really stemmed from its exceptional leaders: Henry Royce, Claude Johnson and Ernest Hives. They are the heroes of this story.

The Engines Were Rolls Royce

CHAPTER 1

The Two Rs

HENRY ROYCE was a remarkable man. He came of humble stock; his upbringing was typical of a poor family in the late 1880s, struggling against adversity. His education was meager, due partly to his family having to move from one place to another seeking work. Hunger was no stranger to Royce and when he first started work, the poor wages combined with long working hours left little over for food or clothes, leisure or relaxation. He was spurred on by a burning desire to help support his family and to gain engineering knowledge and experience. Among his various jobs in these formative years was telegraph messenger boy in London; later on, he sold newspapers for W. H. Smith and Sons; and when times got better, he became an apprentice in a railroad works.

Electricity held a fascination for Royce and so he later found a job with the Electric Light and Power company in London. He was now able to find time to study at the Polytechnic College and so added theory to practice. He met a youth of his own age, one A. E. Claremont and the two combined their savings, some eighty pounds (four hundred dollars) to form a partnership as electricians making small electrical components. It was at this time that the desire for engineering perfection, which later became an obsession, became manifest in Royce.

A company, F. H. Royce and Company, was formed in Manchester in 1884 with Royce and Claremont as partners, and they started on the road to success. Engineering generally was in an early stage and there was much scope for improvement and innovation. Royce made a "breakthrough" by designing a sparkless commutator for dynamos which resulted in their lasting much longer than the ones in general use. This led to manufacturing dynamos for industrial use, which in turn developed into producing the "Royce" electric crane. Quality was the watchword of this company and when competitors started to undercut their prices, Royce would not lower his standards; thus was his reputation enhanced and his pattern for the future firmly set.

Henry Royce had purchased a secondhand Decauville motor car built in France. He soon set about improving it! He decided that there was so much to be done to overcome the little car's deficiencies that he would design a better car, starting from scratch with a clean sheet of paper. He called together his partner Claremont and his two apprentices Haldenby and Platford and announced he was going to build a new "Royce" car. They were, so the story goes, quite flabbergasted, but knowing the boss they acquiesced.

Royce's first little car, which emerged in the spring of 1904, had a two-cylinder engine of ten horsepower. The best features of contemporary cars were embodied and improved upon. Such things as ignition and carburation were inefficient and unreliable at this time, so Royce decided to design his own. The principle on which his carburetor worked remained the Rolls-Royce standard for many years and his custom-made ignition was a great success. From then on, all components of the car except spark plugs, magnetos and batteries were designed and built by Rolls-Royce. These included bakelite mouldings, carburetors, coils, distributors, dynamos, self-starters and so on; only in this way could Royce be satisfied with the standard of quality he insisted upon.

Royce insisted on perfection to a degree that even some of his closest associates thought beyond the bounds of reason and quite impractical if value engineering was to be considered. Nevertheless perfection was the right formula and it was the secret of the rapid success of the early motor cars.

The Hon. Charles S. Rolls was a very colorful character, being an aristocrat, the third son of Lord Llangattock, owner of a considerable estate in Monmouthshire. Having been to Eton College and then taken an engineering degree at Cambridge University, Rolls became interested in the rapidly developing motor car business. He at first concentrated on entering speed trials, at which he soon gained a reputation as a successful competitor. He also became interested in flying both in balloons and powered aircraft. He met the Wright brothers when they were in Europe and bought one of their aeroplanes. (It was in this aircraft that he met his death at age thirty-three, in July 1910, when competing in a spot-landing competition at Bournemouth. When he pulled the stick back to pull out of a dive before landing, a sharp crack was heard and a structural failure caused Rolls's biplane to plunge into the ground, killing him almost instantly.)

Rolls had won many motoring events including the Tourist Trophy in a twenty horsepower Rolls-Royce and had also won events at the Empire City Track at New York. Finally he held the World's Land Speed record at ninety-three miles per hour, won in a seventy-horsepower Mors.

In 1902 Rolls had also started a company in conjunction with Claude Johnson, called C. S. Rolls & Co., selling only quality cars to the wealthy and discriminating motorist. Unfortunately, there were few British cars of quality available owing to earlier "red flag" speed restrictions on cars in Britain. Those on the continent had outstripped the British motor car manufacturers in development. Rolls therefore sold mostly French cars to his friends of wealth and to aristocrats. He deplored this situation and was forever on the lookout for a suitable British car to sell.

The time came when Rolls heard of the little Royce car and its outstanding quality and reliability. He was told about it in 1904 by his friend Henry Edmunds, a keen motorist and a director of Royce, Ltd. in Manchester, who owned the third Royce car to be produced. Rolls was reluctantly prevailed upon by Edmunds to travel to Manchester to go for a trial run in the little two-cylinder car. Rolls had a poor opinion of two-cylinder engines, considering them rough and prone to vibration. However, he was duly impressed by the trial run, saying the little car was as smooth as a four-cylinder one.

Rolls became so enthusiastic that when he returned to London that night, he visited his partner Claude Johnson and hauled him out of bed in the middle of the night to go for a run round the West End of London. Claude Johnson also fell under the spell of the little ten-horsepower car.

Arrangements were quickly put in hand for drafting an agreement between the two companies whereby C. S. Rolls & Company would take the entire output of motor cars from Royce Ltd.! Claude Johnson provided the balance between Rolls and Royce. He was the first secretary of the newly formed Royal Automobile Club, having the reputation of being a brilliant organizer; thus the engineering genius of Henry Royce coupled with the flair for demonstration of the Honorable Charles S. Rolls was channeled into sound business lines by Claude Johnson. These three became the nucleus of Rolls-Royce Ltd., and Royce's old partner A. E. Claremont became chairman.

Now that the first Royce car had been born, several new models were produced to follow the little ten-horsepower model; a fifteen-horsepower, three-cylinder engine was quickly followed by a four-cylinder, twenty-horsepower one, then six-cylinder, thirty-horsepower and finally the famous Silver Ghost 40/50 in 1906. Under the guidance of Claude Johnson as the commercial wizard and the Hon. C. S. Rolls as the sportsman, racing driver and aviator, the cars were entered in competitions and trials. They performed with remarkable success, due, of course, to their reliability and meticulous preparation.

Within only three years, the name of Rolls-Royce was challenging the well-established names of Mercedes, Napier, Daimler and Darracq. By 1911 the product was acknowledged as the "Best Car in the World" and has remained so to this day. There can only be one "best" and that one will continue to sell as long as it remains the best. Hence the continued success of the present Rolls-Royce Motors Ltd.

It is appropriate at this point to mention how Ernest Hives became involved with the company. Young Hives found his opportunity when he was working in a bicycle shop in Reading as a lad. One day in 1901 near closing time, the Hon. C. S. Rolls pulled up driving one of his French motor cars. He had some trouble with the car—a common occurrence in those days—and he needed mechanical help. The owner of the shop said he was closing for the night and could not help. Young Ernest Hives then appeared and asked if he could help. He set to work and soon fixed the trouble: Charles Rolls was impressed and asked young Hives if he would like to come to London to look after his cars and be his personal mechanic. Ernest asked his mother's permission and it was given, so there and then he got into the car and accompanied Rolls back to his home in London.

Hives was thus serving as Rolls's mechanic when Rolls met Royce; then Hives graduated to running the Lillie Hall Service Depot for the new company, Rolls-Royce, Ltd. Hives never looked back and was always proud that he had been a mechanic!

By 1908, the little Cook Street factory in Manchester had been outgrown, and the firm moved to Derby. As it had been decided to build a new factory, Royce designed the layout and buildings which are still being worked efficiently today; such was the foresight of the man.

Royce assumed the role of works director and chief engineer of the company once in Derby. His passion for accuracy and superb workmanship tended on occasion to upset the smooth running of an orderly organization. The legend has been handed down that as he was walking round the factory, if he saw some workman maltreating a tool or saw a part being made incorrectly, he would personally intervene to the discomfort of the person involved.

By 1910, many years of hard work and long hours had taken their toll of the great man's health. Royce was then advised to leave the Midlands and after a long illness from which he nearly died, he was prevailed upon to spend the summers first in St. Margaret's Bay in Kent and then in Sussex, and the winters in the south of France. So drawing offices were built in each place, a small staff of his closest engineers was assembled and it was from these two offices that the original designs were initiated. The designs were sent to Derby to the main drawing offices to be detailed and blueprints prepared. Experimental cars were taken to him for approval. This state of affairs lasted until Royce's death in 1933.

The guidelines for quality engineering had been firmly set. After Royce's death A. G. Elliott, who had been his chief assistant, assumed the mantle of chief engineer. He perpetuated the Royce doctrine of design excellence; he in his turn was replaced many years later by his understudy Arthur Rubbra as watchdog on design. So the quality and attention to detail has been jealously guarded and conscientiously maintained.

Based on the reliability, silence and general refinement of the car, sales promotion to the aristocracy was accomplished as a result of the social connections of Rolls and Claude Johnson; thus the car and the company were firmly established by the time World War I began in 1914.

CHAPTER 2

World War I

WHEN World War I began on August 4, 1914, production of Rolls-Royce cars ceased at the Derby factory, except for a small number which were converted into armored cars. This came about after a group of Rolls owners got together and formed the Royal Automobile Club Corps. There were twenty-five members, mostly titled gentlemen, and they were led by the Duke of Westminster.

These gentlemen offered their cars and their services to the War Office for action in France. They were accepted and so they went over with their cars and were assigned to drive General French and his staff. Soon they were in action doing sterling work, providing rapid and reliable transportation from one headquarters to another in this fluid and fast-moving early phase of the war. They were particularly useful in warding off bands of Uhlans (German cavalry) that went marauding far and wide ahead of the main force.

The need became clear for an armored car that could carry a machine gun and be protected in its vital parts by armor plate and light armament. The springs had to be strengthened, increased cooling provided and other minor modifications incorporated. A number of these armored cars were put through the Rolls-Royce factory and delivered to various nations of the world, including those in West Africa, East Africa, Egypt and Libya. Perhaps the most famous squadron was that led by Lawrence of Arabia in his struggle to unite the Arabs in fighting the Turks in Mesopotamia. One episode stands out and may be taken as typical. A German Mercedes staff car with four German officers aboard was spied by a patrolling Rolls armored car, which immediately gave chase. After a long pursuit across the desert, the Rolls gradually came within range and with a burst of bullets pierced the German car's gasoline tank. The Mercedes came to a halt and the four German officers were duly taken prisoner.

Meanwhile, the Derby factory was required by the government to manufacture aero engines. At this time there was no Rolls-Royce aero engine. Neither Claude Johnson nor Charlie Rolls had been able to persuade "Old Man" Royce to become interested in air transportation. So when the government said the factory would have to make some engines of French design and also one designed by the British government, Royce was incensed and said he would not have his people making engines that did not conform to his own engineering principles. He would, therefore, design one himself, but until it was ready he would agree to help out with what the government wanted.

Royce went to work and with A. G. Elliott, his chief assistant, he designed what he considered to be the right engine. They chose a liquid cooled twelve-cylinder of twenty liters capacity, having two banks of six separate cylinders set at sixty degrees. The cylinders had sheet metal water jackets welded around them. Two inclined valves per cylinder were operated by shaft-driven overhead camshafts. An epicyclic reduction gear was fitted. The engine's total weight was nine hundred pounds and 225 brake horsepower was produced— twenty-five horsepower more than Royce had expected!

This engine had been designed and built in under six months; two years later it had been developed to give 360 brake horsepower. The engine was named the Eagle, the first of a long line of

Rolls-Royce engines named after birds of prey. The Eagle went into production and was ordered by the Air Ministry in large numbers. It was used to power several new aeroplanes, the most prominent being the F.E. 2b, which was highly successful as a fighter. Later the Eagle was used to engine the Handley-Page o/400 bomber, the Fairey IIIF seaplane, the Martinside Rolls-Rayner and the most famous of them all—the Vickers Vimy, which in 1919 was the first aeroplane to make a nonstop crossing of the North Atlantic.

The smaller Falcon of similar specifications to the Eagle came next, but developing 240 brake horsepower. It was required for the Bristol Fighter airplane, which in its turn became one of the most important and successful fighters in the war. Then the Hawk was developed. This engine had six cylinders of the same general configuration as the others except that it was a straight six. It developed seventy-five horsepower and was built especially for a naval nonrigid airship called the Blimp. About seventy-five of these airships were built and used for convoy patrol and general North Sea patrol duties.

Rolls-Royce supplied over 60 percent of all the British-built engines active in World War I; of these, the Eagle was the most universally used. It was decided that production of the Eagle engine parts should be arranged in the United States; then the parts would be shipped back to the United Kingdom for assembly. However, the war came to an end before these parts could be turned into engines. I well remember having to remachine some Eagle valve guides to meet the Rolls-Royce standards when as an apprentice I was going through the machine shops. I can, therefore, claim that I had worked on these old wartime engines both in the shops and on the test beds!

Towards the end of World War I a much larger engine was built—the Condor, of 600/700 horsepower. It was intended to power the Handley-Page V/1500 four-engine bomber whose purpose was to bomb Berlin. (The pilots nicknamed the plane "The Bloody Paralyser.") The war came to an end before this operation could be carried out.

[9]

Several new designs of aero engines were studied at Rolls-Royce during the 1920s; and one or two were made in prototype form, but nothing came of them. The company's main interest was still in the motor car. This lack of enterprise in following up the wartime successes in aero engines allowed rival companies to increase their sales with the new types of aircraft that did appear. Napier offered an aluminum broad arrow layout of 450 horsepower; Bristol, a nine-cylinder air-cooled radial of similar horsepower, and Armstrong-Siddeley had several smaller radial engines from two hundred to four hundred horsepower. The Rolls-Royce Condor of 600 to 700 horsepower was used in some flying boats. There seemed to be scope for a more modern approach to aero engines, but as yet no particular preference had emerged as to which type of engine would be the best to develop.

When it was realized that the end of World War I was not far off, the Rolls-Royce directors had begun to plan for peace and formulate a policy for commercial expansion. No motor car development had been taking place during the war; therefore, the Silver Ghost was still considered sufficiently modern to continue in production for several years. There was a backlog of orders yet to be filled.

The American market was attractive and seemed to be expanding, and there were still parts for Rolls aero engines being made there. Management considered that by making cars in the States, a major market, the company could also circumvent the high protective tariffs levied against imports. All these circumstances decided the company to set up a subsidiary to make an identical car to the ones built at Derby. A factory site at Springfield, Massachusetts, was chosen, skilled fitters and supervisors were sent over, and production got under way.

The company started with a capital of $800,000, the shares being held by the parent company and several American business interests. Altogether 1,703 Silver Ghosts and 1,241 Phantom I's were produced over a period of ten years. At first the chassis were identical and some Derby-built cars were exported to the United States to mingle with American production; but as time went on the

American model diverged from the Derby-built car. Electrical equipment was changed from the Rolls-Royce design to components made by Bosch, and American wire wheels were also fitted. Then many customers began to stipulate that they preferred to buy an imported Derby-built car, and so production dwindled. By 1933 production had ceased. This situation had been accelerated by the Great Depression; in 1933 a few cars were assembled from surplus spares, but in 1934 the company was in the hands of the receiver and in 1935 the factory closed.

Meanwhile, back at Derby two new automobile models had been developed: the Goshawk twenty horsepower and the 40/50 Phantom I. Both were a considerable improvement upon the old Silver Ghost. The experience of developing aero engines during the war had been of value, particularly in producing more power from a given cylinder capacity. So a completely new engine design had come up from Henry Royce's design team.

The Goshawk differed considerably from the Ghost, embodying more up-to-date features; it had a six-cylinder overhead valve engine of just over three liters capacity which gave between fifty and sixty brake horsepower; it was very quiet and smooth running, giving the car a top speed of sixty miles per hour. The distance between the cylinder bores was 4.15 inches; this was decided upon to ensure adequate water space between the cylinders and room for intermediate bearings. It seems to have been a happy choice as this dimension remained unaltered for thirty-seven years. The cylinder bore and piston diameter was three inches. (In the latest version of the basic engine thirty-seven years later, the piston diameter had been increased to 3 ¾ inches with a cylinder capacity of 4.8 liters, giving 215 brake horsepower at forty-two hundred revolutions per minute.) The intention of bringing out a smaller car than the Ghost was mainly to produce a high quality car suitable for an owner-driver. The first models came off the production line without four-wheel brakes; these were later developed and fitted to the last few Silver Ghosts and on later model Goshawks.

In 1925 the Phantom I made its appearance, superceding the

Ghost. The Phantom I had an overhead valve engine similar to the engine of the Goshawk but larger, having a cylinder capacity of 7.7 liters and giving around one hundred brake horsepower. This gave the car a top speed of seventy-five to eighty miles per hour, a considerable advance on the side-valve Ghost which only did about sixty-eight to seventy miles per hour.

The Phantom I was, I considered, a splendid car. Of course, I was very inexperienced when I was made an assistant tester, just having completed my apprenticeship. The Silver Ghost to me, because it had side valves, was a very old-fashioned thing, and being a student of progress, I felt that only overhead valves were any good, preferably operated by overhead camshafts, like contemporary racing cars! So the Phantom, I thought, was a fine old chariot and to be able to drive at eighty miles per hour was quite something. I did on occasion drive the little Goshawks and found them delightfully smooth and quiet and docile; so docile in fact that my little eight-horsepower Talbot was nearly as fast. A good one would do sixty miles per hour!

In the 1920s, the output of both the Goshawk and the Phantom at the Derby factory was steady, at an average of thirty-five cars per week. The work force was now close to four thousand people; the one-pound shares stood at thirty two shillings, a 10 percent dividend was being paid, and everybody was happy. The aero engine business was rather in the doldrums, however, as there were few orders, due to the RAF having run down after the war.

Some two thousand Phantom I's were produced between 1925 and 1929. Then the Phantom II appeared and was produced until 1935; having an aluminum cylinder head with improved porting, it was an improvement on the Mark I. The separate gearbox was discarded in favor of a combined engine and gearbox similar to the twenty-horsepower car; it had semi-eliptic rear springs and hotchkiss drive transmission. Approximately seventeen hundred were produced before it was superceded by the Phantom III. I was still an assistant tester on the Phantom II and thoroughly enjoyed every minute of preparing the cars and taking them out on the road; on occasion, one came up against a worthy opponent to spar with. I remember one day when a three-liter Sunbeam overtook me on the Derby to Buxton road and so I gave chase and we had a ding-dong battle. There was not much to choose between us, the Sunbeam was faster on top speed but the Phantom had better acceleration.

All cars were custom ordered and since the job cards bore the customers' names, the cars were referred to by their future owners' names as they progressed along the assembly line. These names read like a page out of Debrett's Peerage: His Royal Highness the Prince of Wales, Lord Dalmeny, the Duke of Westminster, the Maharajah of Patiala, and so on. It was 1930 before a slump came and a stock of cars built up without any owners' name upon them. These, however, were quickly sold later on, when conditions returned to normal.

The Great Depression affected all motor car manufacturers. Due to reduction in orders, I and several of my colleagues were laid off. I had an interview with Mr. W. O. Bentley, hoping he might give me a job as a tester, but his company was in the same position as Rolls-Royce. He very politely told me he had no vacancy and, in fact, was in a more serious predicament than my old firm. Bentley survived until 1931 before going into the hands of the receiver.

Rolls-Royce production had got going again by that time. The slump was now receding and, since it was the best car in the world, sales were picking up. There was rivalry from Napier, who wanted to get back into luxury motor cars, having been out of the market for some time: they had been concentrating on aero engines with great success.

Napier had nearly finalized a deal to buy up Bentley when, dramatically, Rolls-Royce made a higher bid and clinched the deal. Having beaten Napier to the post, Rolls-Royce didn't know what to do with their new acquisition. I remember meeting W. O. Bentley again: I had returned to the company on the aero side and was in the experimental department where he was working, it having been taken over as part of the Bentley assets! He remembered me from our previous encounter and was amused at the turn things had taken in such a short time.

Rolls did not want to perpetuate the Bentley sports car. Although it was very popular and successful, having built up a reputation as the finest sports car and having won at Le Mans so many times; the Bentley sports car was not in keeping with the tradition of silence and docility, upon which Rolls had built up its reputation. But Hives had a brainstorm; he put the twenty-five-horsepower engine into a Peregrine chassis and this became the Rolls-Bentley silent sports car, with a very good and competitive performance. (The Peregrine was experimental, a delightful little car, having a six-cylinder, sixteen-horsepower engine. Several of them were made, but it was discontinued as they would have been nearly as expensive to produce as the Goshawk.) The marriage of the twenty-five-horsepower engine to the small and lighter chassis with the addition of the Bentley radiator was a stroke of genius and Hives's common sense; and so the modern Bentley was evolved.

At the time, I owned a three-liter Alpine Austro-Daimler, considered a high performance car. I asked Hives if he would like to compare it with the Bentley, so he sent Grylls out with me to try them together on the Uttoxeter straight mile. We tried them for top speed and acceleration, and the Bentley was the better on both counts. The Bentley in the hands of Captain George Eyston, a well-known racing driver, lapped Brooklands at over 120 miles per hour and completed 114.7 miles in the hour. Mr. E. R. Hall owned a Bentley and ran it in the Tourist Trophy races and came in second for three years running.

Before leaving the motor car scene till the end of the war, I must not neglect to mention the Phantom III; this monster superceded the Mark II in 1936 and was discontinued in 1939, when the war started. It had a twelve-cylinder V engine in two banks of six cylinders set at an angle of sixty degrees. It was highly complex and expensive but elegant in the extreme.

In the earlier days of the company, there seemed to be time for a certain amount of practical joking, some of it of quite elaborate nature. One example comes to mind. The company buyer by name Royce, but no relation to the founder of the company, was very keen on riding and went fox hunting. Often on Saturdays, he would come to work wearing his riding habit, top hat and breeches and boots. One day two jokers decided to play a prank on him; they undid the harness of the local milk cart pony and led him to Mr. Royce's office. After some difficulty, they managed to get the horse safely behind the door to await the arrival of the occupant. History does not record further details, which are best left to the imagination! Quite a number of similar escapades took place about this time in the late 1920s but, as the company expanded, life became more serious and jokes less numerous.

CHAPTER 3

A Wise Decision

I HAD joined the Rolls-Royce firm as a premium apprentice in 1925, straight from my boarding school, Shrewsbury. There was an annual intake of twelve such premium apprentices, so called because our parents had to pay four hundred pounds (two thousand dollars) for the privilege of having us taught all the production processes. We spent at least one month in each department, including all types of machine shops, foundries, the laboratory, the hardening and heat treatment shops, and received instruction concerning the drop-forge and finally the fitting and testing of both cars and aero engines. In the evenings we attended the polytechnic to learn drawing and theory, so that at the end of the four years we were well versed in quality engineering.

When I had been at school, I remember well one day walking along near the playing fields thinking what a lucky chap I was. Here I was at one of the finest schools in England; what kind and thoughtful parents I had to have the foresight to send me there at some expense.

I thought I would like to go in for law when I left Shrewsbury and went as far as passing the preliminary examination. My brother, who had also been to Shrewsbury, had decided to go into automobile engineering; soon I had caught the bug from him and so we decided to do the same thing. Influenced by the fact that Major Segrave had just won the French Grand Prix in a Sunbeam racing car, we both wanted to join the Sunbeam automotive company. But Father, who was a doctor and a pioneer motorist, told us that if we wanted to go into engineering there was only one firm to join—the best one—and that would be Rolls-Royce! How wise he was! I have been eternally grateful for his wise counsel ever since.

When we came home for the holidays from Derby, Father used to say with pride to his friends at dinner, "The boys are with Rolls-Royce; apart from cars they make aero engines. Hawkers and people make the wings and things." Years later, when I would be lunching at Hawkers and having a particularly difficult time parrying thrusts from some of their officials about the alleged shortcomings of my company, I was able to recount this story. This would set them back a bit, putting them into the category of builders of gliders and certainly reliant on the engine-builder! For in spite of working on what we thought of as rather old-fashioned side-valve "old ladies' cars," one soon felt the pursuit of excellence in all the processes and in the quality of the engineering at Rolls-Royce. When the overhead valve Phantom car materialized, and as one became familiar with the higher powered aero engines, the feeling of being associated with obsolete "old ladies' cars" engines was dissipated.

One of the things that impressed me as a Rolls-Royce apprentice was the family feeling within the company. Most of the workers had been there for a long time; people never left Rolls-Royce, because they were happy and proud to be associated with the firm. There were a number of other well-known engineering works in Derby, among them the Midland Railway works—much bigger than Rolls-Royce—and Fletchers, International Combustion, Ewart Chain Belt and Aytons, but the workers at Rolls felt rather superior and were proud to be connected with "Royce's." There were never any strikes. There were periods of short-time working and lots of overtime, depending on the industrial situation; in fact, sometimes the company was known as "Rush 'em and Rest 'em"! But it was a very happy organization on the whole.

We premium apprentices aspired to get into the test department and be able to drive the cars on test. I can remember the very first time I drove a Phantom chassis; it was almost, but not quite, as exciting as my first flight as a test pilot. There was a program of tests which each chassis went through before it was sent to the coach builders to have its custom-built body fitted. The engine, after initial assembly, was "run in" burning local town gas for six hours. After this, it was put on a dynamometer test and a complete power curve check was run through, taking another six hours. If these tests were satisfactory, the first road test was carried out by the tester and his assistant, who had prepared the car by checking the controls and making sure there was oil, water and fuel. Judging by today's standards, it seems rather an extravagant procedure, but it surely did ensure a very high standard of quality engineering.

The first road test consisted of a fifty-to-sixty mile run over a routine course consisting of three tests hills which had to be climbed within a certain time at a certain speed. Note was taken of gearbox and back axle noise; if there was any doubt about these components not reaching the required standard of silence the foreman of the fitting shop was taken out for a run, and it was the tester's job to convince him that the noise level was not acceptable and the car would have to go back for improvement. It was often difficult to convince the foreman, since it could affect the weekly bonus for his fitters!

Having completed this test, the engine was decarbonized, then tuned up more carefully and the chassis taken out again on its first final test; this was a run of about thirty miles, up some of the same test hills once more. It would be a check on any components that had to be changed. The engine would again be tuned and then taken out on its second final test. Upon satisfying the tester, the chassis would be handed over to the chief tester, who would give it a short final and then pass it off to the quality tester, who was a member of the inspection department. He in his turn would give it a short run, and when he was satisfied the chassis would be prepared for dispatch by rail to the bodybuilders to have the body fitted. After this, the complete car would have a final test run just to make sure that the fitting of the body had not adversely affected the performance or silence.

Sometime during my apprenticeship in 1926, an unfamiliar exhaust noise began to come continuously from the aero engine test beds. It was quite unlike the normal muted boom coming from the slow-revving Eagles and Condors, which had their exhausts silenced. This new sound was much more like that of a racing car, higher revving and with open stub exhausts. It came from the experimental test bed, which was out of bounds to the general workers. By peeping through a crack in the fence, I was able to see what this new engine looked like, while it was running on the test stand. It was a V-twelve cylinder engine, all aluminum and elegant, and much smaller and more compact than the other aero engines. It looked to be a great improvement on the older engines.

This was the first Falcon X, later to be known as the Kestrel. It started life at 450 brake horsepower and finished up giving 680 brake horsepower. It became the selected engine for most of the new aircraft for the Royal Air Force and the Royal Navy, as well as for numerous foreign aeroplanes. It was, in fact, the ancestor of a long line of successful engines which formed the basis of the R (Schneider) engine, from which the Merlin and finally the Griffon stemmed.

It is interesting to trace how the Kestrel first came about. Sir Richard Fairey, head of the aircraft company which bore his name, was noted for producing elegant-looking aeroplanes such as the Fairey IIIF. He favored liquid-cooled engines and had been using the Napier Lion which gave a clean-looking entry and reduced drag compared with contemporary radial engines. Fairey went to the United States on a visit to discuss ideas on future aircraft development and while there, he was shown the Curtiss D-12 engine. This was a neat-looking, all-aluminum V-12 cylinder, liquid-cooled engine of around four hundred brake horsepower.

It seemed to Sir Richard that the Curtiss D-12 was just what he wanted for his next family of fighter aircraft. He bought some of these engines and talked about license manufacture as he contemplated setting up an engine factory back in the United Kingdom. He fitted the D-12 in his new day bomber, the Fairey Fox, and a number of these were ordered by the RAF and allocated to number twelve squadron at Andover. The small frontal area and sharp nose gave the Fairey Fox a clean and streamlined look. Its high performance gave it immunity from attack by the radial-engined fighters of the day; in fact, it started a new era in aircraft design.

When Sir Richard approached the Air Ministry for official support for his new aero engine company, he learned that they were unwilling to encourage another engine company, there being already four major ones: Rolls-Royce, Napier, Bristol and Armstrong-Siddeley. Air Chief Marshal Sir Geoffrey Salmond, who was air member for Supply and Organization, decided that the right thing to do was to send a D-12 engine up to Rolls-Royce for examination, expecting that a new engine would benefit from some of the up-to-date features of the American engine. Coincidentally Mr. A. J. Rowledge, one of the most talented engine designers in Britain, who had already designed the Napier Lion, had joined Rolls-Royce. So he, working in conjunction with Royce's team at West Wittering, designed the F engine or Kestrel embodying the all-aluminum concept but including detail design philosophy based on the experience gained by previous successful aero engines.

The Kestrel was developed first as a naturally aspirated engine for day bombers and later as a supercharged engine for fighters. The Air Ministry was very satisfied with the initial tests and ordered a batch of engines; these were to be fitted into many new aircraft designs which were now on the drawing board to meet various Air Ministry specifications. Following the initial success of the Fairey Fox day bomber a specification had been written around it, and competition was keen to meet the Air Ministry's need for new aircraft. Fairey entered the Fox but with the Rolls-Royce engine, as the D-12 was now superceded; Hawker Aircraft was offering the Hart, also fitted with the Rolls-Royce Kestrel.

Hawker won the contract and the Hart was built in large numbers for the RAF and later also for export. There were a number of derivatives, for example, the Audax, which was adapted for army cooperation; the Demon, a two-seat fighter with a supercharged engine; and the Hardy, which was an all-purpose bomber for use in India. The Osprey was the naval version. Hawker also won the interceptor order with the Fury and the naval version, the Nimrod; these were very advanced for their time and were the most elegant of all, with fine flying qualities which became very popular in the service.

It was very unfortunate that the Fairey company could not secure any of these orders as they had been the prime movers in introducing the sharp-nosed aircraft. They did, however, obtain a substantial order from Belgium for both the Kestrel-engined Fox and the single-seat Firefly, both aircraft having narrowly missed being selected for the British order.

The various types of Kestrel engine were made in large numbers and fitted in many different aeroplanes, including fighters, bombers, flying boats and float planes. The Germans bought twenty-five of them but they were not allowed to be fitted with the gun interrupter gear because the Treaty of Versailles precluded them from having military equipment. Many years later it was learned that a Kestrel had been fitted for trials in the German Me 109 World War II fighter! The Kestrel gained a high reputation for performance and reliability, its only weak point being a propensity for internal water leaks; these occurred at the top cylinder joint between the cylinder liner joint and the aluminum cylinder block. It was a weak feature in the design which persisted right on into the Merlin and was only really overcome when a two-piece cylinder was developed having a dry joint between the cylinder head and the block. Fortunately, the effect of an internal coolant was not damaging to the engine nor dangerous to the pilot or aircraft. While the engine was operating at power the leak was not apparent. But when the engine was throttled back and the pressure in the cylinder dropped, the coolant would seep into the cylinder, shorting out the spark plugs; so when the engine was again opened up, it misfired on the cylinders affected. This meant that, on landing, the cylinder block would have to be changed.

Much valuable information was obtained from the operation of all these engines in their various airframes. A large service organization had to be set up to make sure that the customers had the service they needed, and Rolls-Royce was once again in the forefront of aviation.

In 1927, when I was yet an apprentice, my father took me to the RAF air pageant and I saw the various Kestrel-engined aircraft performing, notably the Fairey Fox and the Westland Wizard. They out-flew everything else; the normal squadron fighters were slow in comparison. From that day, I became determined to learn to fly. My secret ambition became to fly fast military aircraft, with a remote cherished hope of taking part in the RAF Hendon pageant. It all seemed to be quite impossible, but it was my dream. In actual fact it all happened and more—within ten years I was taking part in the display and was earning my bread and butter as the first test pilot to be on the Rolls-Royce payroll. I even had the experience of flying faster aeroplanes than any others in the country, because our test aircraft had higher powered experimental engines than the normal ones in service.

I finished my apprenticeship in 1929 and became an assistant tester on the Phantom car, a most interesting and enjoyable experience. My pay averaged four pounds (twenty dollars) per week. Alas, it came to an end all too soon in 1930 when the 1929–30 world slump in trade began. This slump affected America rather more than it did the United Kingdom; but it was bad enough, causing unemployment and economic depression.

The immediate effect on Rolls-Royce was that orders for motor cars were cancelled. In order to avoid layoffs as much as possible, production was maintained, but at a lower rate. This resulted in a stock of cars without owners' names on the job cards, as had been the previous custom. The management must have been worried at the time; but not for long, as orders came in again when the crisis was resolved. This recession did not affect the aero engine business as much, since the ongoing orders for the RAF were not changed and plenty of Kestrels were leaving the factory; however, a circumstance did arise which, but for the philanthropy of Lady Houston, could have had the most far-reaching effect not only on Britain, but on the whole world. Such are the imponderables by which, perhaps through lack of imagination, politicians are able to affect the future in most disastrous ways.

CHAPTER 4

Schneider Trophy Race

$\mathbf{A}$S a test driver during a time when no new cars were being developed at Rolls-Royce, I was one who was laid off during the 1929 slump. Being made redundant came as rather a shock to me; there was no certainty that I would be able to resume my career at Rolls-Royce and as there was a general trade depression, I wondered how I would get another job.

I went back home to Newcastle and while making strenuous efforts to find a job in the motor industry, I decided to join the Newcastle Aero Club and learn to fly. I seriously contemplated joining the Royal Air Force on a short service commission, but my father talked me out of it. Once again I took his advice as he had certainly counseled me wisely five years before about joining the Rolls-Royce company rather than Sunbeam.

The nearest I came to getting a job at this time was an offer from Aston-Martin to buy one of their cars at trade discount and a commission on any cars I could sell, but of course "we can't pay you anything," wrote the sales director! I tried W. O. Bentley, who built a rival car to the Rolls, but they were in the same situation; then I approached George Eyston, who was making a name for himself breaking motor car records and winning races. He was developing the power plus supercharger, but alas he could not help either, although he was very kind and sympathetic.

While all this job-hunting was going on and when I had completed my flying course, a letter arrived from Cyril Lovesey, the chief development engineer of the R engine, asking me to go back to Derby to join his team. This came about as a result of the change of mind about competing in the 1931 Schneider Trophy aero race. I was delighted and immediately went back to have an interview and see what job I was expected to do.

Great Britain had won the international Schneider Trophy Race (held every two years) in 1927 with the Supermarine S-5, using a Napier Lion racing engine. The Air Ministry had decided to defend the trophy in 1929. Both the Supermarine and the Gloster aircraft companies decided to build special seaplanes for the race. Gloster decided to use the Napier engine that had won the race previously, as the manufacturers had promised to develop more power. Supermarine, on the other hand, after discussions with Royce and Rowledge agreed to use a new Rolls-Royce engine which was to be developed from the nine hundred horsepower Buzzard. They promised they could obtain fifteen hundred horsepower.

Hives produced this new engine, to be known as the R engine, in three months and it gave 1,545 horsepower on its initial test run. Just two weeks before the race eighteen hundred horsepower was recorded, and on the actual day of the race, the R engine achieved nineteen hundred horsepower. The engine weighed only 1,530 pounds, and this was by far the highest power-to-weight ratio yet achieved with an aero engine. The 1929 race was thus duly won for Britain by Flight Lieutenant Waghorn at a speed of 328.6 miles per hour.

The race was due to be run next in 1931 and if Great Britain were to win again, the trophy could be kept forever. But shortly after the 1929 victory had been gained, the Air Ministry had announced that it would not fund any further development for an aircraft or engine to compete in the next race. This decision was due to the slump which had hit the country at the time, and it seemed a not momentous issue; yet as it turned out, it was crucial in that it may have decided the outcome of the Battle of Britain—to be fought eleven years later! For the lessons learned from the intensive development of the R racing engine aided the development of the Merlin engine which followed.

The Merlin had such inherent strength and technology that it was able to produce more than double the horsepower at the end of the war than it could at the beginning; thus it was able to outperform its adversary. Had all been left to the 1929 decision of the government, this opportunity in development would have been lost; for the intensive work was applied not only to the engine, but to the airframe also. Here the lessons learned were of great value in the ultimate design of the Spitfire.

Fortunately in 1929, the press took up the shortsightedness of the government's decision not to compete in the Schneider Race, and the nation became worried. Within a few months the public-spirited and philanthropic Lady Houston stepped into the breach; she informed the prime minister that she would contribute from her own personal fortune the sum of one hundred thousand pounds (five hundred thousand dollars) over and above what could be provided by the Royal Aero Club. The Air Ministry was thus persuaded to provide the machine and the pilots, since the Royal Aero Club would guarantee the expenses involved. It was settled, and plans to go ahead and develop the new aeroplanes in time for the next contest were set in motion.

As the R engine was to be used once again in the 1931 Schneider Race, urgent development work was proceeding on it in preparation for the next contest. Back at Derby, I was assigned as an assistant to Bob Young, who was conducting tests on a single-cylinder R engine unit; the object was to develop the cylinder to produce as much power as possible by testing various designs of valves, spark plugs, fuels, pistons, etc. It was cheaper and quicker to do the tests on a single-cylinder unit than on the main twelve-cylinder engine. This was of absorbing interest and most instructive.

Taking part in the development of the R engine was an unforgettable experience, and for a young and enthusiastic engineer one could hardly hope for anything more exciting. I have already mentioned that the R engine was a direct development of the H engine or Buzzard, which in turn was a scaled-up version of the Kestrel that had by now gained a high reputation in the armed service.

The R engine was lightened in every possible way by using magnesium castings in nonhighly stressed areas; the cam covers were designed to conform with the cowling lines of the aircraft and the internal working parts were also strengthened. The boost pressure and power output were limited by detonation and preignition caused by red hot valves; special fuels were evolved by Rod Banks, a fuel expert associated with the Ethyl Export Corporation.

The horsepower developed for the 1929 race was 1900, but this was not considered adequate for the 1931 contest. Better fuels were blended and in conjunction with sodium-cooled valves a higher boost pressure was possible, resulting in the power being increased to twenty-three hundred horsepower. This improvement in power increased the stresses in the reciprocating parts; these in turn gave trouble and had to be strengthened. The intention was to establish a reasonable margin of safety for the race by completing a one-hour run at full power.

An example of the kind of problem solving we had to do concerned preignition by the exhaust valves. Those used in the 1929 engine were solid stemmed, made from KE-965 steel. As the throttle was opened and the boost pressure increased, one could see the exhaust valves glow red, then turn bright red, and suddenly with a loud bang the engine would preignite and stop. By adding more methanol to the fuel the valves kept cooler until a higher power was reached, but then pre-ignition would again become apparent. Sodium-cooled valves were tried next; as the heat was conducted away more effectively, they remained black and so the problem of pre-ignition was overcome. Then we found that with various additions of tetra-ethyl-lead and alcohol fuel, the engine could run continuously at plus-eighteen pounds boost, giving twenty-three hundred brake horsepower.

The next problem was to demonstrate that the engine would keep going for an hour. I was assisting on the test bed on the day we tried to complete the test.

All went well until fifty-eight minutes was reached, then there was a loud bang and the engine stopped; a large hole appeared in the crankcase and a large chunk of red hot, twisted connecting rod appeared on the test bed floor! There was only a few weeks to go before the race—and the connecting rod had to be redesigned. On another test one hundred and nineteen gallons of oil was used in an hour, most of it coming out of the crankcase breather. This was brought back within bounds by a redesign of piston and rings. Finally all these difficulties were overcome and a one-hour test run was completed successfully just a few days before the race.

Britain won the 1931 Schneider Trophy Race once again, and so she retained the trophy in perpetuity. Then it was decided to improve the world's speed record. The R engine was further boosted and finally 2783 brake horsepower was developed; with this engine Flight Lieutenant Stainforth raised the speed record to 407.5 miles per hour. This was the end of the power development of the R engine. The High Speed Flight group was disbanded and the aircraft and engines put into storage. Soon, however, some famous sporting enthusiasts saw the possibilities of using these engines to break speed records on land and water. Sir Henry Segrave was the first, obtaining two R engines for use in his boat Miss England. Rolls-Royce took no active part in these tests except for lending the services of mechanics and helping to manufacture some of the difficult installation items.

Segrave was successful in raising the water speed record to 98.76 miles per hour, having done 101.1 miles per hour in one direction, thus becoming the first man to exceed 100 miles per hour on water. Very unfortunately, on the next run over the course the boat hit a piece of driftwood which threw it up into the air; it hit the water and sank. Halliwell, the Rolls-Royce mechanic, was drowned and Segrave, badly injured, died two hours later.

The R engine became the one to use for breaking records both on land and water. Sir Malcolm Campbell obtained a number of the engines, installing them in his record-breaking Bluebird boats and Bluebird cars; he made world records with both. Then George Eyston designed his Thunderbolt car with two R engines and with this car he put the record up to 357.5 miles per hour—which was very close to the speed of the Supermarine S-6 during the 1931 Schneider Trophy Race.

The Kestrel engine was used by George Eyston in a car which captured many long-distance records at the Bonneville Salt Flats in Utah. This car was called Speed of the Wind. It captured all records from five hundred to five thousand miles and from three to forty-eight hours at speeds up to 153 miles per hour. The Rolls-Royce engines now held all speed records on air, land and water.

The reader will perhaps recall some of George Eyston's exploits during the period 1930–39 when he held more official speed records than any living man and on all sorts of cars, from the Magic Midget to the World's Land Speed record on Thunderbolt. Officially Captain G. E. T. Eyston, O.B.E., M.C., George contributed a few of his memories of this era:

My first and distant connection with Rolls-Royce engines was during the First World War; it was to organize a bombing raid on the Leval railway junction far behind the enemy lines during the latter part of 1918. This was with aircraft fitted with the Eagle engine and thus a successful sortie, at least as far as reaching the target was concerned, was assured.

Apart from owning Silver Ghost cars in the early 1920s, my real contact with Derby (where the Rolls-Royce headquarters was located) lasted throughout the 1930s, luckily beginning with the acquaintance with Ernest Hives, who took a very live interest in the experimental cars. I went to see him one day, hoping to get hold of a Kestrel engine for my car, Speed of the Wind, with which I hoped to obtain some long-distance world's records in America. He was very interested, and found me one which had been used on the test beds to blow fresh air over the Schneider Trophy R engine during its tests. The problem was: how to install an aero engine in a motor car? Well, with a sump (crankcase) touching the ground! Of course it meant redesigning the whole of the lower half crankcase which I did, but then I had to have parts made. At last a friendly foreman took compassion; he said the job would be done, and if I came one night all the finished articles would be thrown over the factory wall. It all ended well, for the engine did the job required of it and so there was some compensation for the donors. After my interview with Hives, he took me for a trial run in the prototype 3½-liter Rolls-Bentley, the silent sports car, and I was duly impressed.

Hs (as Hives was widely called) seemed to take a keen interest in my successful record-breaking front-wheel-drive car; it was not a new idea, but it gave food for thought as a possibility for increasing passenger capacity. To my utter surprise, I was asked to join Derby for the purpose of what was termed: "Taking off gadgets on what Hs called his "old ladies' cars"! However, this was diplomatically declined and I turned my attention to the acquisition of some of the R-type Schneider engines for my world speed record-breaking Thunderbolt. One of the engines is in the Royal Air Force Museum at Hendon as it held both the air and land ultimate speed records. It's such a pleasure to recount the trust which was placed on an individual commensurate with that accorded to the humblest employee at Rolls-Royce.

The cars Rolls-Royce have produced have given such romantic pleasure to the world—something to take the mind from worldy matters, owned by such a variety of people. Rolls-Royce always made a great contribution to safety;—who could be reckless with their cars—and I found that other road users had the greatest respect.

In the days I ventured into World's Land Speed records with products of the company, one was conscious of the risks vis-a-vis the firm's unique standing. The task was assured by reason of kindly understanding of the Boss in those times. To Hs and his men it earned my life-long gratitude.

(The Kestrel engine Eyston mentions that powered the Speed of the Wind, which took the twelve- and twenty-four-hour records at the Bonneville Salt Flats in Utah, was an old friend of mine!) It was my job during the Schneider R-engine testing to run this engine, which had a propeller fitted to blow clean air through the test house when the R engine was running at full power. It had already done quite a number of hours flying, having been installed in a flying boat; so it was no chicken when it was given to George Eyston.

The chief foreman he describes who helped him with modifying the crankcase was Bob Coverley, who later became general manager of Rotol, which made many of the propellers during the war. Coverley was very autocratic and rather a martinet. If he felt like doing one a favor he did so for the joy of it and he hated to be thanked for it! He did one for me once: making a set of special gears for my brother's racing car and in a hurry. When I attempted to show my appreciation, he was very abrupt, saying he did it because he wanted to and not to gain thanks!

Speed of the Wind averaged 162.5 miles per hour to beat the world's hour record and then went on to take all records up to twenty-four hours with speeds above 150 miles per hour. George had Chris Staniland, the Fairey test pilot, and Albert Denley as codrivers.

Following these records, the next target was the ultimate land speed record which was then held by Sir Malcolm Campbell in his Blue Bird (which used an R engine) also at 301 miles per hour. George Eyston decided to use two R engines in his own car design, the mighty Thunderbolt. These two engines already had a history behind them, one had twice held the air speed record and the other had been in the S-6 when it won the Schneider Trophy outright.

Eyston says in his recent book *Safety Last:* "The engines proved to be marvelous. They were never bench-tested before I used them, but Rolls sent down two mechanics to examine and reassemble them in my own workshop. Of course it's quite a thrill sitting in a car some thirty-six feet long and weighing about seven tons. Something has got to happen! First time out of the crate, Thunderbold did 352 miles per hour; the return run seemed quicker but the light ray timing apparatus failed! A new attempt was made and an average speed of 345 miles per hour was recorded and duly was registered as the new World's Speed Record." (He then improved it to 357.5 miles per hour.)

George was also an aviator who used to own his own airplanes to fly about the country to expedite his journeys and save time; he last flew a Moth seaplane at the age of seventy. Although I met him on several occasions since the first time when I went to him for a job in 1931, I really got to know him as a fisherman; we regularly go salmon and trout fishing together and I may say he is just as dedicated to this as he was to motoring.

Today, incidentally, the R engines that remain are housed in the Science Museum in London and in the Royal Air Force Museum at Hendon, where they are a great attraction to school boys and enthusiasts. Looking back now, I think perhaps there is a lesson to be learned for politicians in the story of the famous "Racing engine," but then I think there are always lessons for them to learn! We owe all to the public-spirited attitude of Lady Houston for circumventing the penny-pinching policy of the government then in power; for without this crucial development, the Merlin would not have been able to play the part it did in the approaching conflict. Politicians in democratic countries never seem to appreciate the importance of keeping up defense budgets in time of peace, thus making it so easy for the aggressor nations to prepare for war.

CHAPTER 5

Flight Development

NOW that the Schneider Trophy had been secured and the intensive R engine development had eased off, attention at the Derby plant was paid to improving the Kestrel which was in general use in the Royal Air Force. It was realized that experience gained on the R engine could be incorporated in the Kestrel. Many of the Kestrel's defects in service were attributable to the installation. The "plumbing" was left to the aircraft manufacturers, who all employed different cooling and oil systems; some were better than others but all of them had problems—and when a failure took place, the engine got the blame. There were thirteen different firms using the Kestrel in their aeroplanes so it is easy to imagine what a variety of installations there were.

Rolls-Royce decided that it was high time that they took on the responsibility of controlling the installation of their engines. It was also appreciated that testing an engine on the test bed was only half the story and that the behavior in flight was of utmost importance also. Flight testing at that time was being carried out by the various aircraft constructors as and when they wished; such tests came secondary to the development of the airframe. The Royal Aircraft Establishment at Farnborough, run by the government, also carried out engine flight tests, where all engines were tested in various aircraft. Much useful work was carried out here and important results were obtained.

I was sent down to Farnborough, the Air Ministry Research and Development Center, to be the Rolls-Royce representative in monitoring the tests and to keep liaison between the Royal Aircraft Establishment and Rolls-Royce at Derby. I also had to visit the aeroplane companies to coordinate their work. Building on my test bed experiences, I found this work even more interesting.

Sir Henry Royce had died in 1933. He left a legacy of engineering excellence and perfection above all things; on these precepts the success of the company had been built. Now that he was gone, his able designers and engineers, imbued with the great man's engineering principles, carried on. A. G. Elliott and A. J. Rowledge looked after design; and Hives in charge of the experimental department turned their designs into hardware, assisted by Bob Coverley who was in charge of the experimental workshop.

This was the era of the Kestrel going into RAF service, and the development of the Phantom and Bentley cars. Some young and well-qualified engineers, fresh from universities, joined the company; they formed a nucleus of talent for the future in design and development engineering. Senior among these was Cyril Lovesey, who with Arthur Rubbra had joined in 1925; Arthur Rowbotham who had been a premium apprentice became Hives's assistant on the car side. Others were Ray Dorey, Bob Young, Llewellyn Smith, Jim Pearson, while later came David Huddie and Claude Birch; also Stuart Tressillian and Harry Grylls.

There had been a gap in the continuity of recruitment of talent due to World War I, but this late influx of new blood was soon inculcated with the traditions and aims of the company. Most of these young men were later to rise to the top jobs in engineering and management. In 1936 Arthur Wormald died; as a toolmaker, he had been one of the original members of Royce's team in Manchester. When the firm came to Derby in 1908 he was made works manager, which post he held until his death in 1936.

His place was taken by Hives, who was elected to the board and assumed the title of general manager of the whole company. This was an exceedingly wise decision on the part of the board. Hives was universally respected and liked and had all the traditions of the company firmly instilled in his being, while he brought with him his own brand of personality. He combined great charm with a generous spirit and high quality of leadership with an insatiable appetite for hard work. He was respected throughout the industry and highly regarded by the air marshals and top civil servants. He had a large family, both boys and girls, to whom he was devoted. What better ingredients could one have to be in charge of Rolls-Royce at a time of expansion and with the war clouds again looming on the horizon?

We who had been his assistants in the experimental department were delighted. Under Hives's long leadership, Rolls-Royce expanded greatly; the work force rose from approximately four thousand to fifty thousand people and the reputation of the company rose to heights quite unprecedented, both with motor cars and aero engines. With new scientific inventions rapidly spurred on by the possibility of war, Hives eventually led the company into involvement with nuclear energy, gas turbines, industrial and marine engineering, new materials, computers, etc. So in the early 1930s under his dynamic and benevolent leadership, we were all set to go.

During the period when I was at Farnborough, Hives sent for me one day and said that Rowledge wanted me to assist him in developing an automatic control system for the Goshawk engine back at Derby. The Goshawk was a development from the Kestrel, intended to run under steam cooling conditions. I felt very much out of my depth in this assignment, and did not feel competent to be of much use. In fact, I did not want to leave Farnborough just then, as I had just become engaged to a girl who lived there!

After I had studied the problem, I found that there was already an automatic ignition control unit on the market; as a boost control had already been fitted to the Goshawk, what we really needed most was an altitude control and a device for enriching the fuel as the boost pressure increased. I remembered that there was a device called the "Penn altitude control," which I had seen at the RAE; in fact, one had been fitted on a Kestrel and also on a Bristol Jupiter.

I decided to visit Bristol to find out what they were doing. While I was discussing the problem with George Chick, Bristol's service manager, into the office bounced a man with a carburetor in his arms. This was Mr. Davy of S.U. Carburetor Co. Ltd., a lively and energetic man full of ideas who also possessed a sense of fun. He started telling us both how his carburetor worked; how there was one capsule which controlled the mixture with altitude by operating a tapered needle and another one which enrichened the mixture with increase in boost pressure by the same means. The carburetor also had an accelerator pump, which ensured rapid acceleration.

This is just what the doctor ordered, I thought, and I asked Mr. Davy to come up to Derby and see Hives and Lovesey to tell them all about his carburetor. I suddenly happily realized that all these various gadgets which already existed could be incorporated into the Goshawk engine, and that this would be the answer to the need for an automatic control system.

Davy duly arrived a few days later and when he had demonstrated how the carburetor worked, I said I thought that this was the answer. Hives remarked, "They won't let us get away with this," meaning the designers would want something new off the drawing board, and purely Rolls-Royce. But Lovesey ordered two carburetors suitable for the Kestrel which showed up very well on test; we confirmed it in flight and so this carburetor was further developed and adopted for the new Merlin, which was then on the drawing board. The Goshawk engine did not in the end go into production because steam cooling was later abandoned; the Kestrel remained the prime engine until the arrival of the Merlin. I was delighted at the outcome of my little strategem, for I was then able to return to Farnborough, get married, and then go to Hucknall with my bride to start serious test flying.

Ever since that day at Hendon with my father I had wanted to become a test pilot. Having just learned to fly I felt I was getting nearer to my ambition, but it still seemed a very long way off.

It was now 1932, and Hives had put Cyril Lovesey in charge of all aero engine development; Lovesey was a pilot who owned his own De Havilland Moth. He persuaded the Air Ministry to allocate to Rolls-Royce two aircraft for engine testing: a Hawker Horsley and a Fairey IIIF. A Buzzard engine was installed in the Horsley and a Kestrel in the IIIF. These two aircraft were based at Tollerton aerodrome near Nottingham and were operated by the Nottingham flying club whose chief instructor Captain Ronnie Shepherd did the flying. This was the beginning.

By this time I had joined the Royal Auxiliary Air Force in 504 Squadron based at Hucknall near Nottingham and had learned to fly for the second time; I was awarded my wings and flew service type aircraft weekends.

The Royal Auxiliary Air Force was formed in the late 1920s to supplement the regular air force. The idea behind it was the training of volunteer pilots and air crews to full operational standard by forming squadrons using service aircraft. Most of the training was to take place on weekends, while air firing and bombing exercises were scheduled for the annual camp. The commanding officer was chosen from the local gentry, usually a man wealthy, well known and keen on aviation. He was assisted by a regular air force adjutant and an assistant adjutant who acted as instructors. There was also a nucleus of regular airmen to do the aircraft servicing during the week. The pilots, too, were recruited from local sources; they were businessmen, engineers, lawyers and accountants and all had to be keen on attending squadron meetings regularly for training. The air crew too came from local factories and shops and offices. The squadrons were situated near large cities and took the name of the city or country; there were four London squadrons, one at Bristol, and others throughout the country; the one I joined was the County of Nottingham Squadron. These squadrons saved the Air Ministry a lot of money in peacetime. When a national emergency arose, the auxiliary squadrons were expected to become fully operational within a few months, and this is what happened at the beginning of the war.

Joining the auxiliary air force was not always easy because they were a rather select group of people, but it was a very good way of learning to fly properly and to fly service-type military aircraft.

I was putting in as much time as I could flying and even bought a small single-seat monoplane, a DH-53 Humming Bird, in which I toured the country, getting more hours in. My idea was to apply as soon as possible as a test pilot! Eventually, my approval came through and Hives said I could fly the Rolls-Royce test aircraft. So I became the first test pilot on the Rolls-Royce payroll at four pounds, ten shillings ($22.50) a week!

Shortly after this, it was decided that the company should set up a flight test establishment of its own, and so a hangar was leased from the RAF at Hucknall. Shepherd was taken on as chief and I was number two.

Hives gave me the job of developing the steam-cooled system on the Gloster Gnatsnapper. This was a single-seat fighter with a Kestrel engine. Cooling drag was eliminated by dispensing with the radiator and using leading edge surface condensers on the top wing; there was an auxiliary retractable honeycomb condenser for use on climb. The engine ran under boiling conditions; the steam was ducted to the wing condensers, the condensate being returned to the engine by a pump. The main idea was to reduce drag and be less vulnerable to bullets. Since holes in the condenser would only allow steam to escape, the engine could run much longer than if the water radiator was punctured. It was my job to get this system to work properly.

My first flight in the Gnatsnapper was my first as a Rolls-Royce test pilot. It was memorable for other reasons, as well! The weather was cloudy and there was a thick industrial haze that reduced visibility to about a quarter of a mile. I took off and climbed to twenty thousand feet. The rate of climb was impressive and I was thrilled also because, at last, my dream had come true. (We did not use oxygen in those days—we didn't trust it!) When I reached eighteen thousand feet, I noticed the red warning light had come on, meaning that water was building up in the condenser and was not being pumped back into the engine. I had to get down and land as quickly as possible, before an internal water leak developed.

I throttled back and glided down; the water-pressure gauge by now showed that there was no circulation. When I went beneath the cloud, I couldn't find the aerodrome because of the haze; I was getting really worried for there were now only seven gallons of fuel left. I didn't want to use much power because with no water circulation the engine would soon seize up. I thought now that after all the efforts I had made to learn to fly—the hours I had put in to obtain approval—that now that my ambition was fulfilled, I would be grounded! However, the aerodrome suddenly loomed beneath me and I turned sharply and put her down. In case of damage to the engine, I didn't bother to taxi in.

Fortunately, the engine was unharmed and all was well; in fact, everybody thought it was rather a useful test flight. Afterwards, I put on my dirty overalls and investigated the cause of the trouble. The procedure then was to design a modification, take it to the experimental workshop and get it made up. It was then fitted to the system and tested on the ground before the aircraft was flown again to see if there was any improvement.

Eventually, we got it to work satisfactorily. My job then was to write the Air Ministry contract report, so that the firm would receive payment. Altogether I found this a most interesting and instructive job. Rolls-Royce was the ideal place for opportunity; the flexible attitude and encouragement shown particularly by Hives percolated down through his staff right to the shop floor. This broad outlook brought out the best in people; he used to say, "There is no fun like work" and at certain times when under stress, "Work till it hurts." A breed of hardworking dedicated men like Swift, Dorey, Hooker, Pearson, Lovesey, Huddie, Lombard, Claude Birch and many others carried the torch; and so it has been ever since.

We used to have difficulty in starting the engine in the Gnatsnapper. No provision had been made in the installation for the fitting of a starting handle, to mate up with the shaft on the engine. The drill was to swing the propeller while the pilot madly turned the hand magneto in the cockpit; the engine usually started but it was a rather dangerous procedure particularly when the ground was slippery; on a six hundred-horsepower engine it took three men to swing the propeller.

Something had to be done; so I went to Bob Coverley, the superintendent of the experimental shop, and asked him to make up a starting handle attachment like that on the Hawker Hart. At the same time I asked him to copy my new roll-type knee pad which George Bulman of Hawkers had given me, since Ronnie Shepherd wanted one like it.

Bob Coverley agreed to do both things. About an hour later a travesty of the knee pad was placed on my desk. It was a wooden tray about eighteen inches long; a boot-polish tin was mounted at one end, with minutes and seconds marked on it to represent a stop watch; at the other end there was a roll of toilet paper with a handle on it to represent the pad. I took it along to his office where he was having a small meeting with some of his foremen and thanked him for doing it so quickly and said I thought it was a little large to get strapped onto my knee, let alone get it into the cockpit! But the toilet paper might come in handy if I got into a spin and couldn't recover! Coverley was furious at my interruption and kicked me out of his office, saying that he never had the thing made and what did I think he did with his valuable time! He there and then refused to do any work on the Gnatsnapper starting handle. I had to see Hives and complain in order to get things going again! Coverley was quite unpredictable but he turned out magnificent work when he felt like it.

CHAPTER **6**

Flight Testing Expands

THERE were just four of us to start with at the Rolls-Royce flight-testing establishment at Hucknall RAF aerodrome: Ronnie Shepherd and myself as pilots, Harold Green, an experienced engine tester, as the chief ground engineer, and Frank Purnell as the rigger. Soon other ground staff arrived from Derby, quickly followed by some mathematicians to do the performance reduction.

More aircraft arrived: two Hawker Harts, one to be steam cooled, the other for engine tests. Then came the P.V.12 Hart with the new P.V.12 engine, the forerunner of the Merlin. This P.V.12 aircraft had a four-bladed propeller, necessary to absorb the 850 horsepower; it was the fastest climbing aeroplane in the country and only beaten for top speed by the high-speed Super Fury, which itself was soon to join us. The next to come was a Hawker Horsley for flight trials of the Merlin engine. The Condor was taken out and the Merlin installed.

The Rolls-Royce area at Hucknall expanded rapidly. A drawing office was set up, then a wind tunnel, machine shop, sheet-metal shop and coppersmiths, canteen, propeller test bed. The installation department, which did all the designs of power plants for the various companies' prototype aircraft destined to use Rolls-Royce engines also moved over to Hucknall.

Much had been learned about engine installation in the three or four years since the Kestrel engine had gone into service. The theory of forward-facing, expanding-air intakes which gave a modicum of boost at high forward speeds had been proved and the ejector exhaust had been demonstrated; in the case of the Merlin-powered Spitfire, this increased the speed eleven miles per hour.

While we had been flying contemporary service aircraft—mostly biplanes which had quite a lot of built-in drag—small differences in performance due to minor improvements in the installation went by almost unnoticed or were considered within the limits of experimental error. Then Cyril Lovesey suggested that the company should purchase the latest and cleanest monoplane available. The RAE at Farnborough had obtained a Northrop monoplane from America which was giving them good results, and Rolls-Royce decided to buy a Heinkel He70 from Germany. This was an aeroplane of very clean design; the Germans had not been allowed to build engines of high power after the last war, due to the restrictions of the Treaty of Versailles, so they had had to pay much attention to improving aerodynamic design to make the most of the power available to them.

The Heinkel He70 was a four-seat mail and passenger aircraft with a crew of two. When it was tested in the wind tunnel the drag at one hundred miles per hour was only seventy pounds. A Kestrel engine was sent over to the Heinkel works at Rostock to be installed; the Germans said it would take two months to do it. On our arrival to pick up the aeroplane, it was noticed that the engine looked rather secondhand! It had been installed and test flown in a Messerschmitt 109 and I believe in a Heinkel 113 fighter in the meantime. The purchase price of the He70 was thirteen thousand pounds!

Herr Otto Cüno, the German test pilot, flew the aircraft over to Hucknall and checked us out on it. This was a delightful aeroplane to fly and so much faster than anything we had been used to; it did over three hundred miles per hour. When changes were made to the installation such as rear facing exhausts and improved radiator cowlings, we immediately were able to register quite large increases in speed.

The Heinkel became a most valuable asset to us. Cüno was an amiable fellow. He stayed with my wife and me in our apartment in Nottingham and we talked about a possible war, but neither of us really believed it would happen in only four years time. I met him after the war and we had dinner together in London. We were then able to exchange experiences. He had become the chief test pilot at the German test center at Rechlin; he told of many rather hair-raising experiences both in his test flying career and when every possible German aeroplane had been pressed into service to try and evacuate the German army from Stalingrad. He had been flying a Focke-Wulf Condor which caught fire; he said they christened them "Dunhill" as they were always catching fire, rather like our Avro Manchester bomber. We also talked about the rivalry between the German fighters and the British and how the engine development was able to keep the British ones ahead. Of course, he wished they had had Merlins.

The Hucknall test establishment kept on growing, and another pilot, Harvey Heyworth, joined us. We received more aeroplanes, some for just a short time since they came to us from the squadrons when they had complaints they couldn't cure themselves: for example, an epidemic cropped up of engines cutting out during a sideslip when coming in to land; this had caused several forced landings. We were able to diagnose and reproduce the trouble, which was due to an imbalance between the two air intakes. After much flying and experimentation, a fix was produced which was then fitted retroactively in the squadrons.

A new power plant was designed embodying the lessons learned from our flight tests, and much progress was made. At first there were criticisms from some of the aircraft builders who still thought they knew more about it than the engine company, but these were gradually overcome and the reputation of Hucknall became firmly established. The success of Hucknall was in great part due to the manager, Ray Dorey; he had been the deputy chief tester on the R engine under Cyril Lovesey. He led the team in the true Rolls-Royce manner: "Work till it hurts." We engine test pilots were soon cut down to size whereas the test pilots employed by the aircraft firms were looked upon as rather special; "Knights of the air" Hives called them and the word *temperamental* was used to describe some of their actions, particularly if they didn't fly when the weather was doubtful. Hives said to us, "Don't forget you are flying testers and not members of the spotted scarf brigade." We didn't mind—we just got on with the job.

Sometimes we had to fly in pretty awful weather. I remember one day: it was the last day before Christmas and some oil temperature figures were needed to complete a report. The weather was very poor, ten-tenths cloud and raining with not much light left on a December afternoon. I agreed to do a climb to twenty thousand feet and asked my observer, one Les Martin, to take the oil temperature readings every thousand feet on the way up and also on the glide down. We managed the flight all right, but it wasn't at all pleasant and we landed just as it was getting dark; as I taxied in I asked if he had got the figures all right. He replied, "Sorry, my mind was on other things, my wife should be having a baby." My feelings can be imagined; but it was all in the day's work.

The Merlin-powered Horsley was now being used for flight testing, and it was necessary to establish that the Merlin engine performed satisfactorily in the air. Any idiosyncrasies were to be noted and passed on to the aircraft companies, who were using the Merlin in their prototypes. The Hurricane and Fairey Battle were just beginning their preliminary flight trials but the Spitfire was not yet ready. We completed one hundred hours intensive flying in six-and-a-half days without any troubles, which got us all off to a good start.

As production of the new Merlin-engined aircraft got under way and squadrons were equipped with them, we were also allotted some of them for development. By this time (1938), aircraft with other engines were coming to us to be re-engined with the Merlin; the Whitley twin-engined bomber was the first. It had used the Armstrong-Siddeley Tiger, but when fitted with the Merlin its performance was greatly improved; the Merlin thus superseded the Tiger and became standard equipment in the squadrons.

Next to follow was the Wellington bomber, which had originally been fitted with the Bristol Pegasus engine; then came the Bristol Beaufighter, which had a complete Rolls-Royce-designed, power-plant fitted. This was not so much a success as the two bombers, for the Merlin was rather underpowered and later the Beaufighter reverted to using Bristol engines. All this progress took place within four years, so the company was now firmly entrenched in both bombers and fighters—there were more Rolls engines than any other kind in the RAF.

The service department, which was so important in making sure that any troubles might be ironed out with the minimum of delay, was also growing. It had been almost nonexistent after the days of the old Eagle engine following the last war; but since the advent of the Kestrel, it had been steadily expanding. Now that the Merlin was reaching the squadrons in greater numbers, the service department had to play an increasingly important part. Valuable experience in looking after the customer had been gained in the early motor car days; this was one of the reasons that the car had gained such a wonderful reputation. These lessons were to be of value in introducing the Merlin, especially because Hives was determined that this engine should be given every chance and that the RAF should be completely satisfied.

There had been a system of employing outside inspectors with the motor car division in the early days, which had been most successful in fostering good relations between the company and the customer. The inspector traveled around in a Rolls-Royce car, visiting the customers and inquiring from them if all was well, or if there was anything that could be done to solve possible problems they may have encountered. Hives thought the time had come to repeat this process with aero engines. He called me in to see him and explained the way in which he thought this should be done.

I was to be the first such "service representative" and was to combine test flying with liaison with the RAF. This seemed completely sensible, as I was a flight lieutenant in the Royal Auxiliary Air Force and also a member of the 504 Fighter Squadron based at Hucknall. I had a foot in both camps, so to speak. My new job consisted of visiting all the Merlin-engined squadrons and lecturing to the pilots on the correct engine-handling procedure, following with the practical flight-testing results gained during my normal test work experience.

Each squadron and flight commander was invited to visit the Rolls-Royce engine works to see for himself all the care that was put into making and testing the engines. They were then entertained at the company's guest house for dinner and invited to stay the night. Hives, Elliott, Lappin, Lovesey, Dorey and myself were the hosts. This procedure got things off to a very good start as company officials and pilots got to know each other. The service engineers and the RAF mechanics and engineering staff also kept in close contact. The result of all this was that when troubles did arise, they could be speedily dealt with, avoiding a bad name for either the engine or the company. The operators knew that they had only to telephone for advice or request a visit either from a senior engineer or a pilot, whichever we thought necessary.

This type of service to the customer expanded greatly: the company kept careful records of failures, which were later analyzed. These formed a comprehensive data bank, most valuable in tracing causes and helping to effect remedies. Also, as we shall see later on, getting to know so many of the RAF and Royal Navy personnel at an early stage became of inestimable value, as these men were promoted and eventually became senior officers. In the meantime, much goodwill was built up and the tradition of company excellence was maintained and kept fresh.

CHAPTER 7

War Clouds Building Up

THE European political atmosphere was beginning to get tense: Germany was making demands on Czechoslovakia. In 1938 Neville Chamberlain, Britain's prime minister, went to Germany to meet Hitler; we were then on the brink of war. Returning, Chamberlain stepped from his plane, waved a piece of paper and said to the assembled crowd: "This is a declaration signed by Herr Hitler and myself. There will be peace in our time." In fact, the declaration gave us only a year's time. This year was most valuable, as all we had in the way of front-line aircraft were a few squadrons of Hurricanes and one squadron of Spitfires; the remainder of Fighter Command was made up of biplanes, Gladiators, Gauntlets, Hawker Demons and Furies. Bomber Command consisted of Blenheims, Battles, Hampdens, Whitleys and Wellingtons. It was realized, fortunately, that we had only a year to reequip with more modern types, so a crash program was got under way and "shadow" factories were set up to produce more aeroplanes, engines and equipment. Rolls-Royce began building a new factory at Crewe and another was started at Glasgow; production was being speeded up.

When war did start, a year later, the front line looked much better; then we were given another six months before the real hot war started. By this time Fighter Command consisted totally of Hurricanes and Spitfires plus a few squadrons of Beaufighters and Defiants for night work. The bombers, too, looked in better shape when the Merlin Whitley went into service, but the new four-engined bombers had not yet appeared except in prototype form.

I temporarily left Rolls-Royce, because I was called up to join my auxiliary RAF squadron, led by Lord Sherwood. The squadron had recently been equipped with Hurricanes. We flew off to our war station at Digby. I had a letter from the company saying that when hostilities were over I could have my job back and that in the meantime, they would make up my flight lieutenant's pay to my Rolls-Royce salary. I thought this very gracious of them and in keeping with the generous and sympathetic treatment one had come to expect at this time. I kept in touch with my colleagues at Hucknall and was able to tell them how our aeroplanes were performing. I also found myself asking when would they be able to give us more performance? We started the war with wooden propellers but within a few months were able to change them to De Havilland (Hamilton Standard) constant speed ones, which improved performance considerably. Special one-hundred-octane fuel was just becoming available from America, which enabled us to increase the boost pressure to plus-twelve pounds for takeoff, giving us 30 percent more power.

I was fortunate to have Lord Sherwood as my commanding officer; he was also joint undersecretary for air which stood me in good stead when I fell foul of the Twelve Group commander Air Vice Marshal Leigh-Mallory. It happened one day at Hucknall on Empire Air Day. On this day there was an air display at most aerodromes in the country to "show the flag" to the members of the public—the taxpayers—to let them see what they were getting for their money. I was selected to do aerobatics; anybody in the crowd if they spent sixpence could call me up on the radio and ask me to do some maneuver of their choice! I had been practicing using the

Hawker Hind, the type of aircraft with which we were equipped, but by Empire Air Day we had started reequipping with the much faster Hawker Hurricane. There had recently been a number of accidents with these aircraft in other squadrons due to pilot inexperience with these fast monoplanes—if one pulled out of a dive too near the ground, it would be too late for recovery.

I went out to my aeroplane and was introduced to the air minister, Sir Kingsley Wood, who was visiting us that day. I remember him saying to me, "Always keep looking upward, my boy" which was rather prophetic! I did mention to my commander, Lord Sherwood, that I thought there was a height restriction for aerobatics, but he said: "Don't worry, we are the auxiliary air force!" I took off and soon received a radio message to do an upward roll, so I dived down to near the ground and did what I was asked to do. This went on many times with loops and rolls, but as the cloud base was only four thousand feet I would not do a spin.

When I landed, an irate squadron leader came up to me and threatened to put me under arrest for contravening height restriction regulations for aerobatics. A court of enquiry was convened to examine the reasons why the height restriction regulations had been broken. This involved the station commander, the adjutant, Lord Sherwood and myself and it went on for several Saturdays, conducted by squadron leader Ronnie Lees, who used to fly down from his base in his new Spitfire. (Many years later he became Air Marshal Sir Ronnie Lees, deputy chief of the Air Staff, and we have been friends all along. He used to say, "Now boys, get your story straight; then call me in and I will write it down.")

A few weeks later, I was summoned to the presence of Air Marshal Leigh-Mallory and was told the verdict was that I had contravened the regulations and was to be severely reprimanded and considered a disgrace to the air force! I said I was sorry if I had broken any rules, but if I had why didn't one of his staff officers call me on the radio and ask me to stop? As far as being a disgrace to the air force, I told him that he must retract that statement or *otherwise* I would sue him for defamation of character. He asked me to go away and come back in an hour's time.

Meanwhile, I telephoned Lord Sherwood at the Air Ministry and told him what had happened. He said, "Don't worry, we are in this together, and there is no disgrace—I will see the air minister." When I went back to see Leigh-Mallory, he had changed his tune somewhat and said he was deleting from his report the bit about disgrace, but the part concerning the contravention of the standing order should stand. This was fair enough.

Not long after this, the war started, my squadron was mobilized, and it came directly under Leigh-Mallory's command; there was no ill feeling and I was promoted to flight lieutenant. Finally, a message came through from the Air Ministry exonerating me for doing unauthorized aerobatics, as I had been in full practice test flying Hurricanes at Rolls-Royce for several months! It was a difficult time while it lasted, but it was good to have friends at court!

Lord Sherwood left us and went full-time to the Air Ministry, to be replaced by Squadron Leader Victor Beamish, a regular officer and one of very high caliber. It was just what we needed, for he was a strict disciplinarian and full of energy; he got the squadron in tip-top operational shape within a few weeks. We were devoted to him and had complete faith in everything he asked us to do. One day we were at our forward base at Wattisham on the coast at readiness to defend convoys and lightships which were frequently attacked by German raiders; the weather was foul—low clouds and pouring rain with poor visibility.

It was beginning to get dark and we had to return to Debden, our main base. I thought the weather was really too bad to go and so did the rest of the squadron, but Victor thought otherwise and he decided to lead us back in squadron formation. We all took off, formed up and headed for home. We were only about one hundred feet at the most above the ground and even then some of us were touching the clouds—too low for any direction-finding on the radio, so we had to rely entirely on Victor.

I am sure that if anyone other than Victor had been leading, some of the less experienced pilots would have broken off and returned to Wattisham; but nobody dared to leave Victor's formation! We did manage to find Debden; but when we broke formation in order to land, there were Hurricanes going in all directions round the circuit, trying not to collide. We were lucky—all went well, but it was a nasty experience.

Night flying was hazardous at this time because there was a complete blackout. It was very difficult to determine the horizon on a dark night and there was no chance of seeing an enemy aircraft; one was much too occupied trying to keep one's own aircraft on an even keel. Because of the blackout, we lost several pilots. It was unnerving to hear them on the radio saying they were in difficulties, then shortly afterwards to see a flash of fire and hear an explosion as the aircraft went into the ground. It was downright wasteful at this stage of the war, when pilots and machines were in such short supply.

After six months in the auxiliary air force squadron, when nothing much had happened except that we had chased a few Heinkel reconnaissance planes and had taken part in some fairly abortive shipping patrols, I received orders to return to Rolls-Royce but to remain in uniform and be available as required.

On my return I found much activity at Hucknall; there were three more test pilots and many more aircraft of all types requiring power plant development. More power was needed to improve the performance of the Hurricane, which was considerably slower than the opposing Me 109. The Spitfire, now that it had the constant speed propeller and due to the availability of the special one-hundred-octane fuel, was not in urgent need of performance improvement.

A two-speed supercharger version of the Merlin was under development at Derby. This gave a worthwhile increase in power for take-off in low gear and enabled the full throttle height to be increased using high gear. Hucknall was asked by the Air Ministry to fit such a supercharged Merlin into a Hurricane. The result was a general improvement in performance, so it was decided to convert a number of Mark I Hurricanes at Hucknall and at the same time Hawker Aircraft would cease building the Mark I and concentrate on the Mark II.

It was now the spring of 1940. There had been little warlike activity either in the air or on the land, although the Royal Navy had been having a very busy time keeping the sea lanes across the Atlantic open and trying to cope with the submarine menace. Suddenly Germany attacked Norway and Denmark, then overran Belgium, Holland and France. The war was becoming distinctly uncomfortable and near to home.

When it was learned that the Panzers had reached the Channel ports and that the British army had to be evacuated from Dunkirk, that France had surrendered, we felt very naked. Soon the German fighters and dive bombers were attacking the shipping passing through the English Channel and the Fighter Command was truly involved. This was phase one of the Battle of Britain.

Fighter Command was short of aircraft already, as there had been serious losses during the evacuation of the army at Dunkirk. Rolls-Royce was asked to start repairing Mark I Hurricanes, as it was vital to try and keep the front line up to strength in anticipation of the coming battle. Hucknall took this job on while at the same time we were working on developing the Mark II version of the Hurricane. All Hucknall aircraft were armed and at times called on to do patrols and interceptions over the Midlands.

Soon the battle developed and the enemy came inland and bombed the docks, then the fighter airfields. The full onslaught was about to take place.

CHAPTER **8**

The Battle of Britain

IT is now generally agreed by military historians that the most critical battle of World War II, and perhaps even of this century, was the contest in 1940 between Britain's Royal Air Force and the Luftwaffe of Nazi Germany. Many historians now rate the Battle of Britain of comparable significance in shaping the course of history to the Battle of Trafalgar (1805) when Admiral Nelson defeated the French and Spanish naval fleets, thus ending the threat of an invasion of England by Napoleon, and to the Battle of Waterloo (1815) which finally put an end to the political ambitions of Emperor Napoleon.

The Royal Air Force won the Battle of Britain by a very narrow margin indeed. Marshal of the Royal Air Force Lord Tedder, who in 1940 was the director general of research and development at the Air Ministry, subsequently said: "Three factors contributed to the British victory—the skill and bravery of the pilots, the Rolls-Royce Merlin engine and the availability of suitable fuel." Geoffrey Lloyd, head of the United Kingdom Oil Control Board, speaking later in Washington when he voiced thanks for American aid, said: ". . . and I think that without [special rich-mixture-response] one hundred octane we should not have won the Battle of Britain. But we had one hundred octane." Another factor not mentioned at the time, because it was highly secret, was the RAF's use of radio location, subsequently to be better known as radar, a name coined from the words Radio Detection And Ranging. It seems evident that had any one of these factors not been available to the RAF in 1940, the three-times numerical advantage of the Germans would have been decisive.

Hitler, having defeated Poland in September 1939 and then Norway, Denmark, Holland, Belgium and France by mid-June 1940, had forced the British army's evacuation from Dunkirk and had fully expected the British to seek terms for peace. However, he was quickly disillusioned, thus leading to his issuing Directive No. 16, dated July 16, 1940, prefaced as follows: "As England, despite her hopeless military situation, still shows no signs of willingness to come to terms, I have decided to prepare and, if necessary, to carry out a landing operation against her. The aim of this operation is to eliminate the English motherland as a base from which war against Germany can be continued and, if necessary, to occupy the country completely."

The planned invasion of England was given the code name "Seelöwe" (Operation Sea Lion). The landing area was to be on the Sussex and Kent beaches between Brighton and Ramsgate. Over two thousand barges were assembled at harbors and inlets along the Belgian and French coasts, together with a fleet of tugs and motorized vessels to transport a force of 260 thousand men, including six Panzer divisions, three motorized and two airborne divisions. The date of the invasion was to have been September 15, by which time the Germans assumed all effective resistance by the RAF would have been eliminated, this being considered an essential requirement for the success of the landing operation. By September 11, the Luftwaffe had failed to gain any measure of air superiority and the invasion was postponed to September 21. However, on September 15 the Luftwaffe suffered its heaviest losses of the campaign, estimated to have been at least three times those of the RAF. A few days later, Hitler postponed Operation Seelöwe indefinitely.

Had the Luftwaffe won the Battle of Britain and maintained air superiority, many military analysts believe Hitler's planned invasion of England would have been successful. The British army had been forced to leave vast quantities of its equipment and material behind at Dunkirk and it is doubtful if in September 1940 it could have successfully resisted the highly efficient, fully equipped and battle-experienced German army, furthermore fully supported by air cover including dive bombers.

With the British Isles occupied, Hitler would then have been virtually emperor of Europe. The campaign against Russia which began June 22, 1941, could have been started much sooner and thus might have resulted in the defeat and capitulation of the USSR. A decisive victory would likely have been gained before the very cold winter—for which the Germans were not prepared—could have come to the aid of the Russians. Certainly, with England occupied by the Germans, and assuming America's entry into the war, an invasion of France, such as the successful landing on the Normandy beaches by the American and British forces in June 1944, would have been impossible without the availability of England as a staging and supply base. In fact, it is very doubtful if the United States would have decided to come into the European war at all.

Much has been written about the details of the Battle of Britain by a number of authors. They mostly dealt with the day to day confrontations between the Luftwaffe and the RAF Spitfires and Hurricanes. They tell of individual combat, the interception of the German air fleets by the squadrons of RAF fighters, the tally of aircraft destroyed and the tactics employed; also, of the violent disagreements between rival senior commanders on both sides, disagreements which, fortunately, were more intense on the German side.

The German strategy was to eliminate the effectiveness of Britain's fighter defenses as a prime objective, and then to mount a large scale air and seaborne landing. Hitler and Reichsmarschall Hermann Goering were confident of success, since German intelligence had assured them of a three-to-one numerical superiority in the air, as well as a slight edge in aircraft performance.

The battle was fought in four phases. Phase One consisted of attacks on shipping in the English Channel. Phase Two was the major assault on factories, oil storage installations and the London docks. Phase Three was the critical period when the Luftwaffe concentrated its attacks on the RAF fighter airfields. Phase Four came after the failure to immobilize the RAF; indiscriminate attacks were then made by day and night on London and other cities. As it turned out, this gave RAF Fighter Command a much needed respite to get itself reoriented and thus Phase Four proved to be a bad tactical error on the part of the Germans.

The outcome of the Battle of Britain was in the balance for thirteen weeks. Many observers, especially in the United States, had been predicting that a contest between the numerically superior and efficient German air force and the Royal Air Force must inevitably result in the defeat of the British. After all, Charles A. Lindbergh, regarded as one of America's leading aviation authorities, had expressed his opinion that the German Luftwaffe, in the event of war, would quickly overwhelm the combined air forces of the countries of Europe. In 1938, Goering had invited Lindbergh during a visit to Germany to inspect the principal aircraft factories and had even allowed him to fly the Luftwaffe's top fighter plane, the Messerschmitt Bf 109. Tremendously impressed by all he had seen in Germany and unimpressed by what he had seen at that time in England, Lindbergh reported his findings and conveyed his opinions to Joseph P. Kennedy, then U.S. ambassador to Britain, who in turn reported back similarly to Washington.

In September 1939, the Luftwaffe virtually annihilated the well trained but poorly equipped Polish air force in less than a week and then in May and June 1940 defeated the combined Dutch, Belgian and French air forces in about three weeks, despite the help of six squadrons of RAF Hurricanes sent to France. When all

French resistance was ended and Hitler's tanks and armored vehicles rumbled into Paris on June 14, most Americans and even many British were convinced that Lindbergh's and Ambassador Kennedy's predictions would be proved right. However, both were to be proved wrong when the RAF defeated the Luftwaffe in the Battle of Britain.

(Discredited and out of favor, Ambassador Kennedy was recalled by President Roosevelt and replaced. Lindbergh, who had returned to the United States in 1939, became deeply involved in the isolationist America First Committee and the No Foreign War Campaign and in April 1941 resigned his colonel's commission in the U.S. Army Air Corps. After serving as a consultant at Henry Ford's Willow Run plant which built Consolidated B-24 bombers, Lindbergh was engaged by the United Aircraft Corporation and served in the Pacific theater as a civilian technical advisor. Nevertheless, he participated in a number of combat operations against the Japanese and is credited with shooting down one enemy plane).

An analysis of the factors which determined the outcome of the Battle of Britain are of great interest. The importance of the radar early warning system, the cool and determined way in which Air Marshal Sir Hugh Dowding and Air Vice Marshal Sir Keith Park of Fighter Command's Eleven Group husbanded their resources and conducted the battle, and the courage, endurance and skill of the pilots and the ground crews were all indispensable. Nevertheless, the battle could not have been won had not the Merlin engine been capable of achieving a 30 percent increase in power at this crucial time, thereby enabling the British fighters to become superior in performance to the opposing Messerschmitt 109s and 110s.

At the beginning of World War II, the Rolls-Royce Merlin in both the Spitfire and the Hurricane was producing a maximum 1,030 horsepower using eighty-seven-octane fuel (gasoline). The Daimler-Benz DB 601 engine of the Messerschmitt 109 and the twin-engined Messerschmitt 110 produced 1,150 horsepower also using eighty-seven-octane fuel. Information regarding the performance of the Spitfire and the Hurricane obtained by German intelligence in 1938 and 1939 indicated that the Messerschmitt 109 would have the edge on performance, but what the Germans failed to discover until near the end of the Battle of Britain was that every Spitfire and Hurricane was operating with a special grade of one-hundred-octane fuel.

This fuel, imported from the United States and stockpiled by the British Air Ministry just in time for the battle, enabled the supercharger or boost pressure of the Merlin to be raised from plus six pounds per square inch to twelve pounds which increased the power to 1,340 horsepower. This together with the fitting of constant-speed propellers just shortly before the battle greatly improved the performance of the RAF fighters enabling them to deal successfully with the Luftwaffe Messerschmitts, not to mention with the Heinkel and Dornier bombers.

The development of the special one-hundred-octane fuel dated back several years and is a story of its own. The contribution made by the American fuel companies which turned out to be so vital has not been given the credit it deserved. The development of gasoline for aviation piston engines had been taking place since World War I, when it was first discovered that detonation in the cylinders limited the power output and led to failure of the engine. The throttle opening was limited to the point at which detonation began to occur; allowing detonation to persist would result in damage to the engine due to overheating of pistons, valves and spark plugs, leading to preignition and subsequent engine failure.

During the 1930s it was found that by adding between three and four cubic centimeters of tetraethyl lead per gallon of fuel, detonation could be eliminated or at least greatly reduced (depending on the compression ratio or degree of supercharging of the engine). It was also found that aromatic components present in the fuel were superior to naphthenes and paraffins and these could vary appreciably depending on the origin of the crude oil from which the gasoline was refined. While this research was proceeding, partly stimulated by automobile racing and partly by the need to improve the take-off power of aircraft engines, the antiknock value and octane numbers of aviation fuels had been increasing; first, from seventy-four to seventy-seven octane and then following the introduction of tetraethyl lead to eighty-seven octane used by the RAF.

Prior to this, special fuels had been used in small quantities for special purposes, such as the fuel used for the Rolls-Royce R engines in the Schneider Trophy seaplane races. These special fuels were exotic and costly and some contained very little or no conventional gasoline. One blend consisted of 60 percent methyl alcohol, 30 percent benzol and 10 percent acetone with about four cubic centimeters of tetraethyl lead and had an octane number of ninety-five (as measured at lean mixture). The suppression of detonation in this case was mainly due to the high latent heat of vaporization of the methyl alcohol (more than three times that of aviation gasoline).

By 1937, orthodox hydrocarbon fuels had been developed in the United States with an octane number of one hundred (as measured under lean mixture conditions) and were standardized for use in the combat aircraft of the U.S. Army Air Corps. Some of these fuels were tested in British engines, notably the Rolls-Royce Merlin and the Bristol Pegasus, a nine-cylinder, air-cooled radial engine. It was found that different batches of the one-hundred-octane fuel differed widely in antiknock value when the engines were operating at rich mixture under high boost conditions, such as those occurring in combat. Eventually, after a great deal of trial-and-error testing of experimental blends, a suitable one-hundred-octane fuel was found which had the desired rich mixture response.

This blend was evolved by Esso's Research Department (now Exxon) at Bayway, New Jersey, which had developed new methods of refinery processing, including hydrogenation. Credit must be given to Dr. William J. Sweeney who headed the fuels research team there. Credit must also be given to Cyril Lovesey of Rolls-Royce and Harvey Mansell of the Bristol Engine Company who supervised the single-cylinder and full-scale engine testing of the many different samples of one hundred octane that were submitted, mostly by Esso and Shell, for evaluation. Credit is also due to H. C. Tett, W. W. White and Alexander Ogston working with Esso in England and to Ernest Bass of Shell who, working in conjunction with the engine manufacturer, interpreted the test results and transmitted the essential data to America. Much credit, it is now realized, is also due to Major George P. Bulman who from 1928 to 1941 was responsible at the British Air Ministry for engine research and development. Without his support in the granting of development contracts to the engine manufacturers, the Merlin might not have been successfully developed on the special one-hundred-octane fuel in time for the Battle of Britain!

It is of interest to recall that Air Commodore F. R. Banks gave a lecture before the Royal Aeronautical Society in London in 1937 entitled "Some Problems of Modern High-duty Aero Engines and Their Fuels." During the discussion which followed the lecture, the wisdom of developing engines to run on one-hundred-octane fuel was seriously challenged on the grounds that the American sources of supply from which the fuel would have to be imported might not be available in time of war. Banks pointed out that the availability of even a limited supply of one hundred octane might prove decisive in the early stages of a war. His observations were to prove so right just three years later. The first full cargo of the special rich mixture response one-hundred-octane fuel shipped on the S.S. *Beaconhill* tanker from Esso's refinery at Aruba in the West Indies, arrived in Great Britain in June 1939; many others followed and there was an adequate supply just in time for the Battle of Britain.

The misgivings expressed during the discussion following the Banks lecture were not without a certain amount of realism, because on the outbreak of war in September 1939, the U.S. Congress decided that one-hundred-octane aviation fuel was a "strategic material" and, therefore, under the U.S. Neutrality Act could not be exported to any belligerent nation. But a month or so later and by a Rooseveltian compromise, American aviation fuel and other war material could be purchased by Britain on a "cash and carry" basis, provided shipments were made in non-American vessels. This arrangement remained in effect until March 1941 when the Lend-Lease Act became law.

During the Battle of Britain, the consumption of special one hundred octane exceeded all estimates and as the stocks that had been built up rapidly dwindled, barely enough tankers from the United States and the Caribbean reached their destination to replenish supplies and avoid grounding the Hurricanes and Spitfires. The vital importance of tankers to Britain's war effort was clearly apparent to the Germans, whose submarines concentrated their attacks on these vessels. At the height of submarine warfare, one out of every six tankers was being sunk, usually with heavy crew fatalities. Nevertheless, no RAF aircraft was grounded due to lack of one-hundred-octane fuel, a record that was maintained throughout World War II.

The Daimler-Benz DB-601 engines of the Messerschmitts operated on eighty-seven octane gasoline, most of which had been imported from the United States and stockpiled by the Germans before the outbreak of hostilities and the imposition of a blockade by Britain's Royal Navy. Having been taken by surprise by the superior performance of the RAF fighters and especially the Spitfire, the Germans towards the end of the battle introduced to certain squadrons an improved fuel of about ninety-five octane. This was obtained by blending with the eighty-seven-octane fuel a highly aromatic synthetic gasoline manufactured from coal at the hydrogenation plant at the Leuna refinery in eastern Germany. However, as compared with the Merlin, there was not a similar increase in the power of the Daimler-Benz engine. This was presumably due to significant differences between the two engines with regard to valve timing and the fact that the Daimler-Benz was a direct injection engine whereas the Merlin and other British engines used carburetors.

One of the first Spitfire versus Messerschmitt 109 battles took place over Calais in late May 1940. The combat report by the Spitfire pilot, Flight Lieutenant Al Deere, was most valuable as it gave the first accurate assessment of the two aircraft in combat; both pilots were experienced and skillful and thus the respective merits of the two aircraft could be judged. Up until that time, there had been many Hurricane versus Messerschmitt 109 combats in which it was clear that the 109 had a superior performance but was not so maneuverable. It was hoped that the Spitfire would be superior in all respects because it would be providing cover for the Hurricane, which would then concentrate on destroying German bombers.

Al Deere and his Number Two (another Spitfire) had gone across the channel in order to escort a Miles Master training plane which was on a mission to pick up the squadron commander who had previously force landed on an airfield at Calais. Al Deere ordered his Number Two to stay above the clouds to watch out for any enemy aircraft that might try to interfere with the take-off of the Miles Master after picking up the stranded pilot. Al Deere flew low and circled the airfield while the rescue plane took off.

Just at this time, two Messerschmitt 109s appeared and tried to shoot down the little plane which was by now airborne. Al Deere's Spitfire attacked one of the enemy 109s and shot it down into the sea; the other 109 climbed into a cloud, closely followed by Deere. Meanwhile, the other Spitfire was having a very busy time fighting off a number of enemy fighters up above the clouds, which it did successfully.

The individual battle between Deere and his Luftwaffe opponent was one of tight turns, climbs and dives. First, Deere managed to out-turn the 109, which then climbed but could not get away— until it suddenly went into a power dive. This enabled it to draw out of range because when the Spitfire tried to do the same the Merlin engine cut out. As the Spitfire pulled out of the dive, the engine immediately regained power; but Deere then had to catch up with the 109, which he soon did. Repeatedly, a tight turn situation developed, with the Spitfire on the inside of the turn and able to get off a burst from its eight machine guns. The Messerschmitt 109 would again climb and then suddenly dive, leaving the Spitfire out of range. This continued until the Spitfire ran out of ammunition and had to break off the combat and return to base. The superior combat performance and maneuverability of the Spitfire had now been amply demonstrated, but a serious defect of the Merlin engine had also shown up.

We test pilots had complained about this inability of the Merlin to maintain power under negative-G conditions at least a year previously, but at that time the development engineers took little notice! It was not until Squadron Leader Leathart, the commanding officer of Fifty-four Squadron, ran into the same trouble during combat that the importance of this peculiarity became fully appreciated. Leathart flew up to the Rolls-Royce flight test airfield at Hucknall and explained the problems to me in no uncertain terms. I immediately took him over to the main plant at Derby and arranged a meeting with our development engineers. Leathart explained unequivocally that unless a remedy was found very quickly, RAF pilots would be lost and enemy pilots would survive. That did it! An urgent fix was quickly put in hand, first by the Farnborough Royal Aircraft Establishment who tried out a simple restriction in the carburetor fuel line suggested by Miss Schilling, a scientific officer and fuel system specialist who first conceived the idea. It worked by preventing flooding of the carburetor float chamber and momentary cutting out of the engine due to overrichness. Some time after the Battle of Britain, a special negative-G carburetor with a diaphragm instead of a float was put in hand, still later to be superseded by a Bendix carburetor.

CHAPTER 9

Development of Combat Aircraft

Now that the Battle of Britain was over and RAF Fighter Command had won, there were things to be done following the lessons learned in combat. The Hurricane had done sterling work as a bomber destroyer; it had shot down more aircraft in the battle than any other, but most of its targets had been bombers. It was clear that the Hurricane should be developed more for ground attack and as a fighter-bomber. The Merlin 20, two-speed, supercharged engine was adequate for this.

The Spitfire had coped very well against the Messerschmitts. It lent itself more to increases in engine power, because it was lighter and faster and could stay ahead of the German aircraft. This was soon brought home as Fighter Command took the offensive, carrying fighter sweeps over France and acting as escort to Bomber Command in attacking targets just across the channel.

The German Me 109F, it was discovered, had certain improvements that made it more competitive. Lovesey and Hooker had been working hard to improve the Merlin supercharger and came up with a version which fitted to the Merlin, gave 1,470 horsepower at fifteen thousand feet. This engine was called the Merlin 45. The first one was fitted at Hucknall and, after very good results, an order was placed to convert a number of Spitfire I's into Spitfire V's. This model redressed the balance and so honors were roughly even, at least as regards the Me 109F.

The German Focke-Wulf 190, which arrived on the scene some months later, was a very different matter. It was a great improvement over the Me 109. It was fitted with a BMW 801 air-cooled radial engine of seventeen hundred horsepower that gave it a speed of 389 miles per hour at eighteen thousand feet. For a while this outclassed the Spitfire, until once again Lovesey and Hooker came up with the Merlin 66, which had a two-speed, two-stage supercharger and gave 1,720 horsepower. Hucknall again was asked to fit one of these engines in a Spitfire for test. The performance was a great improvement over the Mark V, and gave a speed of 416 miles per hour with a much-improved rate of climb. Again the balance was redressed as the Spitfire with the Merlin 66 was considerably faster than the Focke-Wulf. The Spitfire IX was further developed and so was the FW-190 but the Spitfire stayed ahead.

It was foreseen that there must be an end to the Merlin's development some time, so a larger engine, the Griffon which had the same bore and stroke as the R (Schneider Trophy) engine was developed, and when ready it was fitted in the Spitfire. The Griffon Spitfire 14 had a top speed of 454 miles per hour at twenty-six thousand feet, the engine giving over two thousand horsepower. Thus the British fighters continued to have the edge over the German ones for short-range combat. The fighter sweeps were now beginning to penetrate deeper into enemy territory, escorting the American bombers which were attacking Germany itself. What was needed now was more range, but there were limitations as to what the Spitfire could carry in the way of long-range fuel tanks.

The rapid development of the Merlin which was a vital factor in maintaining Allied air superiority as far as quality and performance went, stemmed from the lessons learned from the R engine and the 1931 Schneider Trophy contest. The basic strength of the component parts of the Merlin engine gave a margin of safety to accommodate the increases in power that would be developed as higher boost pressures became available with the improved fuels necessary to suppress detonation.

The heart of the engine is the supercharger; the good design of this component had been instrumental in the successful performance of the Kestrel engine, the R engine and now the Merlin. Jimmy Ellor and "Prof" Allen were mainly responsible for this and much credit is due to them. Then one day, one of those lucky circumstances happened. Hives had taken on a young and highly qualified Ph.D. graduate from Oxford University, Dr. Stanley Hooker, in order to strengthen his team of development engineers. (Today Sir Stanley Hooker has reached the very top of his profession, having received a knighthood, and amongst many honors has been elected a Fellow of the Royal Society. He is now universally acclaimed as the finest engineer in the business.) In the typical fashion of that time, however, he was put in a small office and left to make his own way without any particular briefing!

After several days of reading the paper and wandering round the factory, which was not a very popular thing to do in those days, particularly in the experimental department—out of bounds to most people—Hooker went into "Prof" Allen's office to find him studying sheafs of figures having to do with supercharger calculations. Hooker asked if he might have a look at them; Allen was only too pleased to show him and tell him what it was all about. This was right up Stanley's street, as it was a subject he understood, having been studying mathematics and aerodynamics at Oxford. He took the calculations back to his little office and after several days wrote a talented report, pointing out where efficiencies could be improved which would in turn enable the engine to produce more power.

A few weeks later, Jimmy Ellor came into Hooker's office waving the report saying, "Did you write this? It is brilliant. I want you to take charge of all supercharger development." Stanley was put into the same office with Cyril Lovesey who, the reader will recall, was in charge of all aero engine development under Hives. This was a happy arrangement as Lovesey was outstanding in his ability in mechanical development of engines. Thus, as Hooker improved the supercharger and its aerodynamics, enabling more power to be obtained, Lovesey ensured that the engine could stand it. The result was a rapid increase in power and at higher altitudes with engine reliability. One wonders what might have happened had young Hooker not come to Rolls-Royce or if he had not been given that particular job. Success seems to depend on such slender chances; perhaps Britain has a guardian angel looking after its welfare!

The Merlin was able to keep ahead of its German contemporaries all the time, the power increasing from one thousand horsepower at the beginning of World War II to over two thousand horsepower at the end! In 1944, when the German V-1 "flying bombs" started coming over, the Mustangs, the Spitfires and Mosquitos, all using Merlin engines but by now using plus twenty-five pounds of boost and giving over two thousand horsepower, were able to intercept and destroy these wicked but ingenious weapons.

While all this fighter development was going on, we had been keeping in close contact with the fighter squadrons and with the Air Fighting Development Unit, which was based at Duxford. This unit, commanded by Wing Commander Ian Campbell-Orde who before the war had been in the Royal Auxiliary Air Force and was therefore a colleague of mine, was formed in order to study fighter tactics and assess the capabilities of all fighters both Allied and enemy when they became available! We always took our latest development aircraft from Hucknall to Duxford for them to fly and form an opinion upon their performance. One day Campbell-Orde rang me up and asked me to fly down and see him. He wanted me to fly a new American aeroplane which had recently arrived in this country; this was the North American Mustang. I was glad to do so and on this day, the concept of the Merlin P-51 Mustang was born.

The history of the Mustang and how it came into being was not a straightforward one. Robert Gruenhagen, in his excellent book called *The Mustang*, describes the earlier history of the plane as follows:

The Mustang, which became the greatest piston-engined fighter ever built, began its career as a fighter nobody wanted, commissioned to meet a British specification in 1940. The RAF were searching the free world for military aircraft to supplement the excellent fighters they already had, but which were in short supply. The U.S. Air Force took such a dim view of an aeroplane not even off the drawing boards that it tried to get North American Aviation, with its superior manufacturing capabilities, to build the Curtiss-Wright P-40 which already existed. But North American stuck to its guns, and in the unbelievable time of sixty-five days, designed and built the airframe of what was considered the most aerodynamically perfect fighter of World War II.

The prototype Mustang first flew on October 26, 1940, and on its fifth test flight it crashed and lay upside down with its back broken in a plowed field just short of the runway of the Los Angeles Airport. Again, the decision had to be made whether to continue building an untested aeroplane or to start immediate production on the Curtiss P-40. North American decided in favor of the Mustang. The Mustang was fitted with an Allison V-1710 twelve-cylinder engine of 1200 horsepower. This engine was the standard American liquid-cooled engine in use in the Curtiss P-40. In general layout it resembled the Merlin but it had a much inferior altitude performance. After some successful trials of the Mustang, it was established that the aircraft's performance and handling were extremely good. An order for several hundred Mustangs was placed by the British government for use in the RAF, for low-level reconaissance and army cooperation. It was one of these Mustangs which I was invited to fly at Duxford, where it was being tested for combat duty.

The first thing I noticed during the flight was that the indicated speed was some thirty miles per hour more at similar power settings than on a Spitfire! The ailerons were light and gave a rapid rate of roll; this was one of the areas where the Focke-Wulf had an advantage over the Spitfire. The guns, too, were close inboard, which gave a concentrated fire, but most important, the internal fuel capacity was three times greater than the Spitfire—which meant that the Mustang would be able to provide an escort to the bombers for deep penetration into Germany. I was very impressed with the aeroplane, which seemed to me to be a natural for the two-speed, two-stage Merlin 66, which was just coming into service on the Spitfire IX. I felt that the Merlin 66 would greatly improve the speed of the Mustang, as its full throttle height would be very much greater than with the Allison engine and the thirty or so miles per hour higher indicated speed maintained at altitude would mean an increase in true speed of perhaps fifty miles per hour! I discussed this all with Campbell-Orde and Ted Smith after the flight and they concurred, so we agreed to try and promote the proposal of re-engining the Mustang with the Merlin.

I went back to Hucknall full of excitement and reported to Ray Dorey, who quickly saw the point. I wrote a report to Hives and other senior officials suggesting this should be done as it would be the answer to the FW 190 and also provide long-range escort for bombers. One of the officials wrote back suggesting that all the Merlin 66s were required for Spitfires and the new bombers, so why waste them on an untried American aeroplane! This was the sort of thing one had sometimes to put up with. It was a clear case of the "NIH factor" (not invented here).

However, I went to see Hives in his office at Derby and with all the enthusiasm and conviction I could muster told him what a splendid aircraft the Mustang was and how it was needed badly in the RAF and could we have one at Hucknall to do a Merlin conversion? He saw the point and then and there telephoned Air Marshall Sir Wilfrid Freeman at the Air Ministry and told him the story, recommending that he authorize three Mustangs to be sent to Hucknall for this purpose. Previous to this meeting I had taken the precaution to ask our performance people to calculate what the performance was likely to be. The answer came back that it would be 50 miles per hour faster and the rate of climb would be much quicker, also with greatly extended range.

Three Allison-engined Mustangs duly arrived a few days later and design work started. The first Merlin installation was completed and flown on October 13, 1942, the work of conversion having started in

August; my initial flight at Duxford was on April 30, so it all happened rather quickly once the go-ahead had been given. It is often the way this sort of thing happens. An idea is born, then people pour cold water on it, time is wasted, opposition mounts up and maybe the whole idea is dropped. It is rather like trying to light a piece of damp paper with a match in a high wind! But once the fire starts and people become interested, it can become a real conflagration! In the case of the Mustang, this is exactly what happened.

The good news of the Merlin Mustang's vastly improved performance spread like wild fire and was conveyed to Washington, whereupon large orders were placed with North American for Merlin Mustangs. Extra factories were built and production was to rise to five hundred per month. Merlin engines were built in the United States in large quantities by Packard and Continental, both for the Mustangs and other aircraft. Over fifteen thousand Mustangs were produced, and the plane was acknowledged to be the most versatile fighter of the war. Marshal Goering is reported to have said when he saw Mustangs escorting American and British bombers over Berlin that he realized Germany had lost the war.

In fact, the U.S. Air Force daylight bombing raids over Germany had been discontinued for a while, due to very heavy losses when they were unescorted. Once the Mustangs became available to escort the bombers all the way, things became very different; the Mustangs were able to protect the bombers and destroy a large number of German fighters while doing so. The Mustang was also indispensable later on in the Pacific war, where long range was an absolute necessity. It was able to carry a great deal of fuel in its long-range drop tanks; under certain circumstances the ferry range was as much as twenty-nine hundred miles.

When the war was over, a number of Mustang long-distance records were set up, the most famous one being the transatlantic crossing flown by the late Captain Charlie Blair in his Mustang, *Excalibur III*. One day in 1951 Captain Blair came to see me in my office on Conduit Street. He said he intended to fly across the

Atlantic, then to cross the North Pole and return to New York via Greenland and Alaska. He was rather worried about how best to operate the Merlin engine for maximum range and how to avoid the plugs leading up when using low power for long-range cruise conditions. I was able to turn up my old figures on range flying which we used during the war in our talks to the squadron pilots.

Captain Blair was at this time the senior pilot on the staff of Pan American World Airways, flying Stratocruisers. He said that he would try out the fuel consumption figures which we had given him on the Mustang and call back to see me after his next trip on Pan Am. About two weeks later, he arrived back in the office and said he had flown the Mustang up to Alaska and back and the figures seemed about right and that by periodically opening up the revolutions per minute he avoided leading up the spark plugs.

A few weeks later, Blair arrived at London Airport in Excalibur III, having flown across the Atlantic in seven hours and forty-eight minutes! He then went on to fly over the North Pole, in ten hours and twenty-nine minutes, landing at Fairbanks, Alaska. He then completed the trip from Fairbanks to New York in nine hours and thirty-one minutes.

The British and Allies now had the clear superiority over the Germans as far as fighters were concerned, at least in the European theater. The improved Spitfires and the Mustang were supreme; they were also supported by Hawker's new aeroplanes: the Typhoon and the Tempest; these were used mostly as fighter bombers and did very good work during the invasion of Europe. They used the twenty-four-cylinder, sleeve-valve H engine, designed and built by Napier. One of the prototypes had been fitted with the Rolls-Royce Vulture engine; this was a twenty-four-cylinder X engine of seventeen hundred horsepower which was designed primarily for the Manchester bomber. The Napier Sabre gave over two thousand horsepower and so was adopted for these fighters.

The situation in the Middle East, however, was very different. The Middle East air force was equipped with Hurricanes and Spitfire Vs. They were up against an odd assortment of Italian fighters which gave them little trouble, but then the Me 109s and FW190s arrived. It was the same story all over again; the Me 109G, which was an improved model after the E and F, was better than the Spitfire V at altitude, but for low altitude operation the FW 190 was used. The combination of these two gave the Hurricanes and Spitfires a bad time, since the Spitfire IX had not yet been assigned to this theater.

Air Vice Marshal Graham Dawson, who was the British command engineer, wrote to Hives and asked him to send somebody out to Egypt to see how things were going from an engine point of view. I was asked to go and see how the Merlins were performing and particularly how they stood up to the sandy desert conditions.

The first problem was how to redress the discrepancy between the Spitfire and the German fighters. The local workshops had been trying to get more power out of the Merlin by setting the propeller to give 3,200 revolutions per minute with no improvement. This was not surprising as the propeller lost efficiency at these revolutions per minute, and the engine power curve peaked between 2,850 and 3,000 revolutions per minute! I sent a cable to Lovesey and Hooker asking them how much should be machined off the supercharger rotor to give plus eighteen pounds of boost at six thousand feet, which was the height at which combat with the FW 190 was taking place. The reply came back "three quarters of an inch." It was arranged to crop three rotors immediately and that I should fly down to Aboukir to test the engines in the air.

The estimate was exactly right and the eighteen pounds of boost materialized at six thousand feet; this, together with an improved air filter and cropped wing tips, which incidentally improved the rate of roll, gave an increased speed of twenty-two miles per hour and also a better climb at low altitude. Resulting from these improvements, a wing of three squadrons was converted and thus was the balance redressed. Curtiss Warhawks were also used in the desert; these were P-40s fitted with American-built Merlin 20 engines and they were halfway between the Spitfire and the Hurricane for performance.

While I was testing one of the converted Spitfire Vs, now known as VBs and the engine the Merlin 45M, the engine suddenly blew up; white smoke came out of the exhaust and the engine lost all power. I force-landed in the desert, radioing for assistance. While waiting for help to arrive, I looked around the aeroplane and noticed the port aileron hanging loose. One of the hinge brackets had fractured. In fact, it had been rather fortunate that the engine had failed, as I had been about to do a vertical dive to test the rate of roll at high speed. This would certainly have pulled the aileron off, which could have been embarrassing.

Soon after this, half the Spitfires were converted; the other half remained as they were to operate at altitude and were able to cope with the Me 109s while the VBs stayed low to deal with the FW 190s. This arrangement worked well.

A visit was made to the Middle East by Air Marshal Sir Trafford Leigh-Mallory, who now headed Fighter Command in England. He was impressed by the low altitude modification on the Merlin and decided to have a number of his Spitfires converted too, which could hold the fort, so to speak, until all his squadrons were equipped with the more modern and superior Mark IXs. When the Air Ministry back home got to know about this unauthorized modification carried out by Dawson's engineers, they were highly critical. Nevertheless, they granted approval and so a number of the older aircraft were modified. This did help the squadrons when pitted against the FW190s.

While I was out in the Middle East an Me 109G was captured intact. Dawson instructed me to fly up to Lydda (the airport for Jerusalem) and test it; he said, "Take Air Marshal Sir Hugh Pugh Lloyd's Hurricane; I will tell him; he won't mind." I duly collected the aeroplane which had the Air Marshal's broad pennant painted on the side and off I went to Jerusalem. I flew the Me 109G and found it very lively but not as pleasant to fly as the Spitfire. It was very interesting to me, however, to be able to compare the two aircraft from a fighting point of view, checking maneuverability, pilot's view and rate of climb, turning circle and the ability of the

From 1884 until 1903, Henry Royce was in business at Cooke Street,
Manchester, manufacturing electrical equipment. After his decision in
1903 to manufacture automobiles and his subsequent agreement with
the Hon. Charles S. Rolls, most of the work at the Cooke premises was
on the production of cars. Early Rolls-Royce cars are seen here in the
assembly shop at Cooke Street.

Henry Royce at his Cooke Street factory in 1904.

The Hon. C. S. Rolls driving a very early twenty-horsepower four-cylinder Rolls-Royce in 1907.

The two-cylinder Royce car, circa 1904.

Ernest W. Hives driving a fifteen-horse-power three-cylinder Rolls-Royce, circa 1909.

The Hon. C. S. Rolls winning the 1906 Tourist Trophy Race on the Isle of Man with the twenty-horsepower Rolls-Royce.

The Hon. C. S. Rolls driving a forty/fifty-horsepower Silver Ghost shortly before his accidental death in 1910.

The Hon. Charles S. Rolls at the controls of his French-built Wright biplane at Bournemouth, England, July 11, 1910. The photograph was taken only a few minutes before the biplane crashed due to a structural failure, fatally injuring Charles Rolls. Just the previous month, Rolls had made the first double crossing of the English Channel and was the first pilot to fly from England to France.

Ernest Hives in the special forty/fifty-horsepower Silver Ghost which he
drove at over one hundred miles per hour at the Brooklands Motor Racing
Track in 1911.

Final assembly line of twenty-horsepower and forty/fifty horse-power cars at the Rolls-Royce plant, Derby, England, in 1924.

Sir Henry Royce at the wheel of a forty/fifty-horsepower Silver Ghost, circa 1925.

The Thunderbolt, driven by Captain G. E. T. (George) Eyston, breaking the World's Speed Record at 357.5 miles per hour at the Bonneville Salt Flats, Utah, 1937. (*Bill Shipler, Salt Lake City*)

(Inset) Captain G. E. T. Eyston, O.B.E., M.C.
(*From the author's personal collection*)

A 1937 4¼-liter (259 cubic inches) Bentley two-door sedan.
(G. Leslie Horn, Enfield, Middlesex; England)

A 1948 Rolls-Royce Silver Wraith.

The 1959 Rolls-Royce Silver Cloud had automatic transmission, power steering, servo-assisted brakes and rear shock absorbers (dampers) with a variable setting controlled by a switch on the steering column.

A Bentley Continental Sports two-door sedan.

The Rolls-Royce Phantom VI presented to Her Majesty Queen
Elizabeth by the Society of Motor Manufacturers and Traders
on the occasion of her 1977 Silver Jubilee.

The author with his Rolls Bentley Continental, late 1960s.
(*From the author's personal collection*)

Rolls-Royce Hawk six-cylinder in line liquid-cooled engine of seventy-
five horsepower, one of the earliest Rolls-Royce aero engines, first
produced in 1915.

A 1978 Rolls-Royce Corniche two-door convertible.

The 1916 Rolls-Royce Falcon of 250 horsepower, which engined
the famous Bristol fighter during World War I.

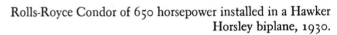

Rolls-Royce Condor of 650 horsepower installed in a Hawker
Horsley biplane, 1930.

Test stand view of the famous R engine which powered the Schneider Trophy
winners for Britain and was a direct forerunner of the Merlin.
(*Support Graphics Ltd.*)

The Supermarine S6B
owered with the R engine
which established a
World's Air Speed Record
f 407.5 miles per hour in
931 when the engine de-
eloped 2,650 horsepower.

The first Kestrel engine
was flight tested in a De
villand DM-9A in 1927.
*From the author's personal
collection)*

The Rolls-Royce Kestrel of 715 horsepower was in production
from 1927 until 1938 and powered over twenty-five different
types of RAF aircraft. It was the original power plant of the
German Messerschmitt 109 prototype.

The Hawker Super Fury powered with the Rolls-Royce Kestrel
was the fastest military airplane in the world in 1934.

Daimler-Benz engine to keep running when upside down. The Allied airplanes that I had flown, and this included the Curtiss Kittyhawk, seemed to be more sophisticated and expensive, whereas the German planes were perhaps more austere and functional and easier to produce in large numbers.

Having flown the Me 109G, I spent the night in Jerusalem with Wing Commander McDonald, a great friend of mine and incidentally godfather to my daughter. We had dinner at the King David Hotel where we witnessed a rather amusing incident: in the cocktail bar we noticed a smart young army officer talking with an attractive young woman, both smartly dressed. Suddenly in came a rather scruffy flying officer straight from the desert in battle dress, which was, to say the least, still bearing traces of sand. He went up to the barman and demanded a Slivovitz; he then took a mouthful and blew it out through his lips, lighting it at the same time so that a long blue flame shot out between the guardee officer and his girlfriend. Contrary to my expectations, they both laughed and thought it a great joke; the guardee then went to the bar and ordered one, but evidently he was given the wrong brand—when he tried to perform, it just dribbled down his tunic with a weak flicker of flame. Everybody roared with laughter and some relief, as we thought there might have been an ugly scene.

The next morning I flew back to Cairo in the Hurricane. I had a shocking hangover, which made the trip highly unpleasant, particularly as most of the way was in a dust storm, and on my landing at Cairo, a tire burst. Next morning, when I turned up at the Middle East Headquarters to report on my flight, I was met on the steps by Group Captain Tyndel-Carrol-Worsley. He said, "For goodness sake, go away for a few days! Hugh Pugh Lloyd is furious and wants to see this Squadron Leader Harker who went off in his Hurricane without permission and just before he himself was going to fly it to visit one of his stations in the desert." It turned out that Air Vice Marshal Dawson had forgotten to get Lloyd's permission to borrow his Hurricane. But when all was explained, I was forgiven this episode and even to this day when I meet Air

Marshal Lloyd, he reminds me of the day I stole his aeroplane.

One of the things that was worrying the planning staff at headquarters just before the battle of Alamein was the persistent overflying of the delta area by high-flying German Junkers 86-P aeroplanes. These could fly above 45,000 feet and the Spitfire IX could not quite reach them. Even back in England, where the Junkers had also been carrying out reconnaissance flights and had dropped a bomb on Bristol, Fighter Command could not do a successful interception.

Air Commodore Smylie, who was in charge of workshops at Aboukir, evolved a plan which turned out to be successful. Two Merlin engines were modified by raising the compression ratio. The cylinder blocks were machined down until the valves hit the pistons so the pistons were scalloped out to give clearance. Smylie happened to have on his staff a Flight Lieutenant Beauchamp who before the war had been a carburetor expert on Cyril Lovesey's development team; he altered the taper on the carburetor needles to give a correct mixture strength at very high altitude and therefore more power. These two engines were installed in two lightened Spitfires, one of which had a radio set and the other only two guns. They were to fly in formation, the one with the radio leading which when in contact would hand over to the one with the guns. They soon had an opportunity to intercept some Junkers by climbing up to over forty-six thousand feet and shooting the enemy down. This deterred the Germans from snooping any more. Once again the ingenuity of the Middle East engineers was able to come up with the answer by exploiting the inherent versatility of the Rolls-Royce Merlin.

There were some remarkable repairs carried out by the engineering workshops in Egypt; this was necessary due to the shortage of aircraft and spare parts. Aircraft had to be ferried out from Britain a long way round, via West Africa; there was then a distance of five thousand miles across the continent. Spare parts came by sea; the trip was very precarious because of enemy submarines. As a result of the shortage of repair materials some ingenious improvisations were contrived; bearing shells were machined from scrap propeller blades, and pistons which had worn were peened over to reduce the clearance. Probably the most serious problem was loss of compression due to sand getting into the engine. It seemed impossible to keep the sand out during a dust storm; air cleaners were provided which were effective during take-off and landing but sand could find its way into the engine through the exhaust ports when the engine was at rest. This reduced the life of the engine considerably.

The pilots and ground staff appreciated the help which Rolls-Royce was able to give. They felt they were not being neglected and so the traditional service and care for the customer was maintained. The ability of the engine to react to exceptional circumstances was once again demonstrated and the foresight of the designers amply demonstrated. The Merlin engine for a fighter aircraft had gained a terrific reputation.

CHAPTER 10

Bombers and Fighters

WHILE The Merlin had been making its vital contribution to improving fighter performance and enabling the British to maintain a definite edge over the enemy, a similar story was unfolding in Bomber Command. This development started before the war, in 1938, when the Armstrong-Whitworth Whitley K-7208 came to Hucknall for the Merlin to be fitted to replace the Siddeley Tiger. Two complete power plants were designed and built at Hucknall, embodying all the latest techniques in power plant engineering gained from experience during flight trials since 1935. The flight trials were very successful with a considerable gain in performance being recorded in all aspects, takeoff distance, load carrying capability and speed at a higher altitude. The Merlin Whitley went into production and became the equipment for number Four Bomber Group based in Yorkshire.

Number Ten Squadron, commanded by Wing Commander Bill Staten, was the first to receive these aircraft. I spent quite a lot of time with the pilots explaining the best method of operation of the engine; they were Merlin 20s with two-speed superchargers; the low-speed gear improved power for take off and the high gear for high altitude cruise. Whitleys had the longest range of the British bombers; they operated at night and were able to penetrate as far as Berlin and Turin. The Vickers Wellington came in for the same treatment and Merlin power plants replaced the Bristol Pegasus or perhaps supplemented them as both types remained in production. Again this was the case with the Bristol Beaufighter. The four-engined bombers which had been designed to an advanced specification were soon to be ready for their first flights. The Short Stirling was to use Bristol engines; the Handley-Page Halifax had Merlin 20s and the Avro Manchester had two Rolls Vultures.

The Halifax and Stirling were able to carry heavy loads of bombs far into enemy territory; they were well protected by turrets of two and four guns and as long as they operated by night they were able to penetrate deeply into enemy territory and drop heavy loads. The Manchester carried comparable bomb loads and was equally effective for awhile, until their losses mounted. This was in part due to the Rolls-Royce Vulture engine, I regret to say. There were certain problems with the cooling system which we at Hucknall were trying to rectify in our flying test bed, the Vulture Henley. There was also a serious problem with connecting rod bearing failures and when these occurred, the engine would catch fire and so the aircraft would be lost.

These troubles were eventually overcome but not before a number of Manchesters had been lost. In fact, I was there when we lost our test aeroplane. I happened to have flown over to Ternhill Aerodrome where I was giving a talk to the pilots of the fighter conversion unit. I was standing on the aerodrome talking to Squadron Leader Gerry Edge who, incidentally, was to become godfather to my second daughter! He was a good friend of mine and I had joined his 605 Squadron at the end of the Battle of Britain, where it was operating from Croydon. It had been the first squadron equipped with the Hurricane Mark II. Group Captain Teddy Donaldson, who was the station commander, was also with us.

We saw a Manchester approaching the aerodrome with one engine on fire. The pilot, Reg Curlew, one of our test pilots, and very experienced on large multiengined aircraft, seemed to be well in control; he was making a downwind approach with enough height, so it seemed, to be able at least to turn and land across-wind. He must have thought he could get round into wind, so he continued the circuit before turning into wind for the final approach. Alas, he undershot and landed just short of the aerodrome in a field which had some large trees in it. He hit one of these and a wing was pulled off, rupturing the fuel tank; there was an explosion and the whole aeroplane went up in flames. We rushed to the spot in the group captain's car only to find a mass of flames; the two flight observers had managed to crawl out of the rear door and were not badly burned but there was no sign of Reg Curlew. Gerry Edge and Teddy Donaldson, amidst the exploding ammunition, did get into the aircraft by the rear door for a few moments. Gerry Edge said he saw the pilot still in his seat but crushed against the control column and obviously either dead or unconscious. One of the tires then burst, the aircraft settled down and another tank burst so Gerry made a hurried retreat, getting out just in the nick of time before the whole thing became one mass of flames.

Hives then made a firm and difficult decision which turned out to be perhaps one of those moments when big issues are decided although not quite realized at the time. He stopped production on the Vulture engine and arranged with Avros to fit four Merlins instead; the Merlins would give more power and be more reliable and also enable the factory to produce more engines by concentrating on only one type. It was a fairly simple modification to the aircraft, really only affecting the wing. The result—the Lancaster, the best bomber of the war without any doubt whatsoever, both in range, speed and load-carrying capacity. As the engine power was developed, the Lancaster was able to take full advantage of it, just as the Spitfire and the Mustang had in the fighter role. The Lancaster by the end of the war was able to carry a twenty thousand-pound bomb like those used to sink the German battleship *Turpitz*.

Rolls-Royce Merlins were now fitted in the Whitley, Wellington,

Halifax and Lancaster aircrafts. We had one of each of these at Hucknall for engine and installation development. We also visited all the bomber squadrons using these aircraft, to be of help and give advice to the pilots on engine operation. We found that individual pilots, not fully understanding the intricacies of engine control and operation, used to think they knew best how to operate the aircraft, with the result that some of them returned poor range figures compared with others. Naturally, it was very important to get the maximum range out of the aircraft and that results should all be consistent. It was clear that there would have to be more care and attention given to pilot training.

Courses were set up at the Rolls-Royce instruction school where pilots were given instruction, as were ground staff, in maintenance. A convincing demonstration that certainly impressed the students was set up on the test bed. The engine would be set to give seven hundred horsepower at maximum cruise revolutions per minute and the pilots asked to look at the flowmeter where they would note the fuel consumption; then the revolutions per minute would be reduced and the boost increased to give the same power; they would look again at the fuel consumption and note the difference! They would note that there was a large saving in fuel by operating at high boost and low revolutions per minute. This doctrine was then instilled in them and gradually uniformity of consumption pre-vailed in the squadrons.

This was an important aspect of service and customer relations, a legacy from the old motor car days! Group Captain Hamish Mahaddie tells an amusing story about when he was given command of a Lancaster squadron and they were engaged on long raids into Italy. He had just been on the Rolls-Royce engine-handling course and had been very impressed by the doctrine of low revolutions per minute and high boost for conserving fuel. He ran a sweepstakes to see which crew could return from each raid with the largest reserve of fuel. He was surprised that he never won! He eventually found out some months afterwards that a certain officer of mid-European descent had been posted from the squadron; he had been the organizer of the sweep which involved each member of the crew putting half a crown into the kitty; as there were eight men in the crew and usually eight aircraft in a squadron raid, that added up to eight pounds to the winning crew! On the return from the raid this officer and a corporal used to dip the fuel tanks; they had a private "deal" going between them, so it transpired that the aircraft in which this officer was flying always won. The corporal was posted to another squadron but before he left he felt he ought to tell his commander about this "fiddle" in the sweepstakes.

The De Havilland Mosquito was the next bomber to come along that was fitted with two Merlins. It was one of those remarkable aeroplanes that had a difficult beginning in life but having started as an unarmed day bomber and photo reconaissance aircraft, it finished as the most successful night fighter, intruder and light bomber. It was able to avoid enemy fighters and to catch enemy bombers. The Mosquito was originally intended to be a light bomber that could outpace enemy fighters. The final design took the form of a twin-engined aircraft of wooden construction and very clean lines, having two side-by-side seats for pilot and navigator. It was powered with two Merlin engines, and relied on speed to keep it out of trouble. After much discussion with the Air Ministry, an order was placed for fifty to contract specification B.1/40. De Havilland pointed out that the design of the aircraft lent itself for further development as a night fighter, but little interest was shown by the ministry at first. However, provision was made in the design for mounting four twenty-millimeter cannons grouped together in the nose. Eventually, it was agreed to include a number of fighter versions in the initial contract.

Many variants were eventually produced, including a Sea Mosquito for the Royal Navy's Fleet Air Arm which carried a torpedo and could be operated from an aircraft carrier. The fighter-bomber version could carry two thousand pounds of bombs and sufficient fuel for long-range while equipped with four cannons and four machine guns. The Mosquito was a most versatile aeroplane and a mix of bombs, guns, rockets and long-range fuel tanks could be fitted, depending on the task to be carried out. They even flew to neutral Sweden to pick up ball bearings, which for a time were in very short supply in England. For the latter operation they were painted in British Overseas Airways Corporation colors and were flown by airline pilots, even a passenger being sometimes carried in a bomb bay! At times, the Mosquitos were intercepted by Focke-Wulf 190s, but they were able to outpace them; none were lost.

British bombing of Germany in the early stages of the war was not very effective as the technique of night bombing operations had not been fully developed; bomb loads were light and there were relatively few bomber aircraft in service. However, as the new heavy four-engine bombers became available and the air war intensified, the RAF mounted retaliatory raids. One such raid is particularly noteworthy. On August 25, 1940, the Luftwaffe dropped some bombs on the city of London; until then German bombing had been confined roughly to military and industrial targets. This raid on a densely populated area of London so enraged Winston Churchill that he ordered a reprisal raid on Berlin. This so annoyed Hitler, who had assured the German people that Berlin would never be bombed, that he switched his bombing attacks from the fighter airfields to bombing London. This was a tactical error as it relieved the pressure on the hard-pressed fighter bases and gave the pilots respite and time to regroup.

As the war progressed, British and American raids on Germany became devastatingly heavy and went on night after night and during the day, but not without serious Allied losses, for the German night fighter defenses had been well developed. Of a big raid on Hamburg when thirty thousand Germans had been killed, Albert Speer, the German minister of construction, remarked after the war that if a raid of this size had been repeated for six nights in a row, Germany would have had to capitulate; unfortunately, since it would have shortened the war, it was not possible. Bomber

Command had lost one thousand bombers during four months in 1944—so the battle was not all one-sided.

The production of Merlins had increased rapidly since the beginning of the war. At first there was only the Derby factory, which was concentrating on supplying engines for fighters; then a new factory was built at Crewe in 1938–39, another at Glasgow in 1939–40; then the Ford Motor Company at Manchester started turning out Merlins. These factories produced engines for the bombers. A team went over to America to arrange license production at Packard and Continental; most of these engines were for the Merlin Mustang and Merlin Warhawk, also for Canadian-built Hurricanes and Mosquitos and Lancasters. Altogether 166 thousand Merlin engines were produced.

While all this intensive development of aero engines and rapidly increased production was taking place, the Rolls-Royce work force, too, was expanding rapidly; it stood at some four thousand people in the 1930s and finished up at the end of the war at forty-seven thousand. This expansion, particularly under wartime conditions, put a great strain on administration and organization.

Hives controlled the whole machine by his ceaseless efforts and example which enabled such remarkable results to be achieved. He kept in close day-to-day touch with all that was going on. He personally paid frequent visits to RAF bases, accompanied by Bill Lappin, his personal assistant; Lappin knew many of the senior officers in the RAF and was able to smooth the way when required. Consequently, Hives was kept fully aware of what the services needed and whether they were satisfied with what they were getting.

Hives had personal charm and was universally popular with all the workers, shop stewards and the works convener, which kept everybody happy, and labor relations were excellent; no such things as strikes or "go-slows" took place. Hives was called Hs from the system of designating two or three letters (usually three) to abbreviate the surnames of his executives—a system unique to Rolls-Royce and one often mentioned as an eccentricity of Hives. Because Hs used to walk around the factory when time permitted, he was a familiar figure to many of the workers in all of the Rolls-Royce factories. He used to hold engine development meetings every Monday afternoon and, of course, many other meetings too; but the development meetings which I was privileged to attend were rather special because he reviewed the state of the Merlin and Griffon engines in service.

He would conduct these development meetings in the board room with most heads of departments present, representing design, production, development, flight test and service complaints. They were very serious meetings, and discussion became quite agitated at times between the various department chiefs; but always Hives calmed everybody down and with his wry smile settled any argument peaceably. He had a fine sense of humor which often asserted itself even when things became serious. I particularly remember two incidents worth recounting.

Witold Challier, our Polish performance expert, was asked by Hives when he would be able to produce some performance estimates for the Spitfire with a certain engine modification. Challier replied he thought he might have the answers ready in a week. This was no good to the Boss who said, "I want them tonight." Challier replied, "Do you expect me to perform miracles?" "Certainly," said Hives, "that is what we pay you for." Challier retorted, "You remember the last person who performed miracles? Well, I don't propose to end up like that!" Hives had the last word and said, "He did them for nothing!"

On another occasion I was dozing off; it was a warm afternoon and I had been flying all morning. Suddenly I heard Hives say, "How is the ATD unit performing?" (ATD was an abbreviation for the automatic timing device on the Griffon engine.) I awoke with a start and said, "I don't know, I haven't visited them recently." There were many units I used to visit, for example, the PRU, the AFDU, and several others, but I was caught by the "ATD unit." Hs didn't mind and everybody laughed, much to my discomfort.

Another occasion demonstrates Hives's sangfroid. I was in his office near the experimental department reporting to him some performance results of one of our aeroplanes when in burst one of the test assistants, who said, "There's a fire in the shop!" Hives said, "Go and put it out," but a few moments later, the man came into the office again and said, "The fire is up to the roof now and has set off the sprinklers. What shall we do?" So again Hives said to go and put it out; but after the third time when the man came in again and said, "It's serious, shall we get the fire brigade?" Hives said to me, "I think we had better go and see what has happened." When we got there the fire was nearly over; it was just some gasoline that had spilled into an inspection pit and someone had thrown in a cigarette end!

When war clouds loomed in 1939 and the company's emphasis was increasingly on developing and producing aero engines, the motor car was relegated to a secondary consideration. Car production ceased, experimental work on a new model came to a halt and the chassis was shipped over to North America to be safe from enemy bombing. Several Bentley B models which would have gone into production were kept for the use of Hives and Sidgreaves, while one was lent to Air Marshal Sir Arthur Harris, the commander-in-chief of Bomber Command.

Most of the personnel from the motor car division were drafted into aero work. A small design team was retained which became involved with the design and development of a forty-millimeter gun and later with tank design in cooperation with Leyland Motors. This activity expanded due to advice being sought on how to make tanks more reliable with more powerful engines. W. A. Rowbotham, who had been a Rolls-Royce premium apprentice several years before me, was in charge; he was seconded to the Ministry of Supply as chief engineer of tank design for the duration of the war.

British tanks at the early part of the war were rather inferior, undergunned, underpowered and not very reliable. Rowbotham and his team were responsible for adapting the Merlin to fit into the Crusader tank that turned out later in the war to be a success. The Rover Car Company took over production of the Merlin Meteor tank engine; it differed from the aero engine in that the supercharger was removed and normal carburetors were fitted, the oil pumps were modified and several other changes were made.

The car design team also designed a range of military gasoline engines for the army; they were based on the car design and came in three sizes: a four-cylinder, a six and an eight, all having common pistons, connecting rods and other common parts. After the war they were made in quantity for several types of army vehicles.

Having concentrated on describing the Merlin in some detail, I now propose to mention some of the other engines which had been built but which were shelved so that full attention could be given to the Merlin and, in some degree, to the Griffon. A. J. Rowledge designed a twenty-four-cylinder, air-cooled, sleeve-valve engine arranged in the form of an **X**. This was intended for use in the Fleet Air Arm; its capacity was 22.1 liters and it developed 920 brake horsepower at eleven thousand feet. It was installed in a Fairey Battle which we used as a test bed at Hucknall. It ran extremely smoothly and was reliable; we did several hundred hours flying with it, using it mostly for transportation because the urgent military need for its development no longer existed.

The Vulture I have already dealt with as an engine for the Manchester bomber and as a possibility for the Hawker Tornado fighter. The Griffon, which was really a scaled-up version of the Merlin, ran in the opposite direction; this at first caused some confusion when it was installed in the Seafire, the naval version of the Spitfire. The Griffon's torque reaction tended to pull the aeroplane in to the "island" (bridge, funnel, etc.) of the aircraft carrier; later, contra-rotating propellers were fitted to overcome this. The Griffon was also fitted in the Mark V Firefly and Barracuda Beaufighter and Shackleton; they were also used in a marine version to propel high-speed air/sea rescue launches.

A very advanced twelve-cylinder, two-stroke, fuel-injection, liquid-cooled engine called the Crecy was built and run; it never reached the flight stage but did give two thousand horsepower on the test bed. The final piston engine, which was discontinued because of the advent of the jet, was the twenty-four-cylinder Eagle of forty-six liters capacity. It had sleeve valves, a two-speed, two-stage supercharger and contra-rotating propellers; it gave thirty-five hundred horsepower. It flew in the Westland Wyvern but was superceded by a turbo-propeller engine. This brings us up to 1943 and the advent of the jet—the beginning of a new era.

CHAPTER 11

Test-Flying Episodes

ALTHOUGH being a test pilot had been my early ambition and it was certainly an exciting job, fortunately remarkably few of the adverse occurrences during my time at Hucknall had serious consequences. This was partly due perhaps to the general reliability of Rolls-Royce engines, in spite of their being mainly experimental. The inspection and maintenance of the airframes and engines backed by the discipline of Ray Dorey, the manager, certainly played an important part. Although we had to fly a great deal, often in bad weather, and we had to conform to the schedule of hard work expected of all employees in the experimental department, our safety record was good.

The first episode I can remember, apart from my initial flight in the Gnatsnapper, was when Ronnie Shepherd was testing some experimental exhausts on a Hawker Hart; kidney-shaped, they were known as the pepper-pot type. There were three of them on each side of the engine, fed from short pipes from each two cylinders. The purpose of these new exhausts was flame suppression for night flying. Shepherd carried out some slow rolls, a maneuver that caused the engine to cut out due to carburetor flooding; raw fuel went through the engine and collected in the pepper-pot kidneys. After several of these rolls, when the engine fired again, the contents of the kidneys lit up, causing a sheet of flame to crawl along the fabric of the fuselage, burning off all the fabric on one side. Fortunately, the elevator surfaces were not damaged and Shepherd was able to fly the aeroplane back to base.

Harvey Heyworth had two forced landings on golf courses, one in the Heinkel after running out of fuel and the other in a Lancaster. He was not popular with the golfers, as more repair work had to be done to the golf courses than to the aeroplanes—which says something for his skill.

Roscoe Turner was flying a Halifax four-engine bomber with a crew of five on board when an engine caught fire. They couldn't put it out so they all abandoned the aircraft—safely, except that Turner's parachute caught fire. This accelerated his rate of descent so that he sustained a broken ankle upon landing.

There was the unfortunate incident of the Manchester, already described in an earlier chapter, when an engine caught fire and was followed by a crash and a flaming landing that caused the death of Reg Curlew. On another occasion, David MacCartney was doing some tests on a negative-G carburetor in a Hurricane when the engine faded out; on the subsequent forced landing the aircraft turned over and caught fire, killing him. There were other fatal accidents and a number of forced landings but, considering the number of hours flown, the record was good.

There were, however, less serious happenings, some quite amusing. On one occasion, bearing failures in fighter aircraft, both Hurricane and Spitfire, were becoming too frequent, causing engine fires and in many cases the loss of the aircraft. At Hives's Monday afternoon development meetings this item had been on the agenda for some time and no amount of discussion had come up with a cure. I said I thought I could reproduce a failure in the air, because it was due to the behavior of the engine in aerobatics! Hives said, "I bet you a pound you can't."

I went back to the aerodrome and arranged a series of tests which

I felt sure would cause a failure. A very severe condition could be imposed on the engine during slow rolls; when the engine was upside down, the engine "cut," the oil pressure fell to zero and the propeller went into fine pitch. On completion of the roll when the power came on again the revolutions per minute would go up to thirty-six hundred with no oil pressure; after a few seconds the engine condition would again stabilize and the revolutions per minute would drop to within limits when the propeller pitch control took over once more. With no oil pressure under these conditions, I was sure the bearings would fail if one repeated the maneuver often enough. But I repeated this exercise 156 times with no trouble.

I then decided to do some vertical dives with a reduced amount of oil in the tank; this resulted in a fluctuating oil pressure using full throttle and thirty-six hundred revolutions per minute for at least a minute on end. I tried this half a dozen times and again no failure. It was then decided to take the engine out and dismantle it for examination, the result being that it was in very good condition! At the next Monday meeting I had to hand over the pound to Lord Hives.

Group Captain Stokes, who joined us later on in the war, had a number of forced landings; one in a Mustang when he was flying it using 102 inches of boost; that was full throttle at sea level in high gear! He was all right but the aircraft was damaged. On another occasion he had ferried a Mosquito out to Turkey; the next day he took up a Turkish general for a demonstration flight. Having feathered one engine, it would not unfeather and, as that engine had the air pump fitted, the brake pressure was not adequate; on landing, the aircraft swung and damaged the landing gear. Stokes sent us back a cryptic telegram: "Slight landing accident, aircraft damaged, ignore rumors." We thought this was very funny, so inserted it in the pilots' "Line Book."

A party of us from Rolls had been invited down to a guest night at Manston to celebrate the formation of the first jet squadron. The following day the weather was appalling, low clouds, rain, poor visibility; I did not want to take off, but Adrian Lombard, always very "press on," said he had to get back to Derby to a meeting. I was flying the Oxford, a twin-engine trainer which had seats for four or five people. None of us except Lombard wanted to leave. We took off and headed north across the Thames estuary, flying about two hundred feet above it; the port engine quit half way across. It is difficult to maintain height with a fully loaded Oxford on one engine, so we edged round to return to Manston and the problem became now how to find it under these weather conditions. We had spotted the approach sodium lights and made a dart for the runway when suddenly a Mosquito flashed past in front of us. We went right into its slipstream, which tipped us up onto one wing at ninety degrees to the runway with only about one hundred feet clear. We slipped towards the ground, just picking the wing up enough before our undercarriage touched with a lot of yaw on. Fortunately, nothing was broken, but we could have lost Lombard, the world's best engine designer.

Harry Bailey, one of our pilots, and I decided we ought to join the navy for a short while to learn how to land on the deck of an aircraft carrier; we had been visiting various carriers, as they were now using our engines in Seafires, Fairey Barracudas and Fireflies. We duly reported for duty at Inskip aerodrome to carry out dummy deck landings, using Sea Hurricanes. The Royal Navy had a special technique for landing on the deck; the aircraft is brought in close to the stall with engine on. The pilot is controlled by the batsman, who is on the deck telling you either to increase power or vice versa, according to altitude, and then when he thinks you are ready to touch down, he gives you the "cut." When we had got the hang of it, we were sent off to land on H.M.S. *Ravager*, a small converted banana boat. Harry made six very good landings while I on my first attempt missed the wires and went through both barriers, pulling off the landing gear and breaking the propeller and, incidentally, tipping up the aircraft ahead of me on the front of the flight deck—a good thing he was there as I should have gone over the bows! After a pink gin in the ward room they sent me off again on our remaining Hurricane and I was able to complete my six landings, so all was well. My wife was having a baby on that very day so I blame that for my untidy performance.

One day I was flying a Hurricane; while on the climb up to cruising altitude an oil pipe came adrift. Soon I was covered in hot oil and the instrument panel was obscured, as were my goggles. Because the inside of the windscreen was becoming opaque, I opened the hood; but this made matters worse due to the suction produced. I lifted my goggles so that I might see out; this let the hot oil into my eyes, which stung and blinded me. I felt now that I was badly placed and wondered whether to bail out. I could no longer control the aeroplane nor did I know where I was, over open country or over a town.

Gradually my eyes cleared as the tear ducts began to wash the oil film away; by then, although my vision was blurred, I could see a little. The next problem was how long the engine would run without any oil. Fortunately, I had not gone very far from the aerodrome, so throttled back and started to descend; I luckily found it and managed to land by looking out over the wing. Having come to a halt, I climbed out onto the wing, which was coated with oil, and promptly slipped off it onto the ground. I sprained my back, which put me in bed for a few days!

I sometimes used to take my miniature dachshund with me when flying the Miles Monarch or Whitney Straight communication planes. On one occasion I remember I was flying fairly close to a Handley-Page Hampden; the little dog spotted it and started barking at it—hard to think what went on in her mind!

There was always some excitement going on, mostly I think due to bad weather and poor visibility at the base, where there was always much smoke from factory chimneys. We all became very good at finding our way home by dead reckoning; there were no aids to navigation until later and no flying control apart from an Aldis lamp or Verey pistols to fire color-cartridges.

Whilst writing about memories both pleasant and interesting, I recall an occasion that shows what an ephemeral thing war and its passions can be, though at the time highly emotional and very serious even unto the final sacrifice. The competition between the design teams of the nations at war was never-ending and no pains were spared to evolve the most ghastly engines of destruction; yet soon after hostilities were ended, a rapport developed between former enemy nations simply through an interest in advancing technology.

This was particularly noticeable in aircraft engineering. It was acknowledged that the Germans had made vast strides in the advancement of aerodynamics and rocketry so that their knowledge was sought after as a matter of urgency, so that such knowledge did not get into the hands of the Soviets. It was fully recognized that although the Russians had been partners in arms they were also a threat to the future; and now that the war was over, there would be a technological race in preparation for another arms build-up between the West and the East. The Americans, fortunately, were able to obtain the services of Dr. von Braun, the German rocket expert who had developed the V-2; this laid the foundation for the American rocket and space programs.

We at Rolls-Royce had been closely involved with the improvement of aircraft by being ahead of the enemy in engine development; it was fully realized that the Germans had been exploring all means to gain superiority in aircraft design, and in some aspects they were more advanced and had covered a wider field of research. In the fighter field this competition had been intense; there had also been a more friendly rivalry at home between Hawker and Supermarine and to some extent Martin-Baker. I thought it would be interesting and of value, as we only produced engines, to have the experts' views on the future, views from both friend and foe sitting round the table in discussion. So I invited Sir Sidney Camm from Hawkers, Joe Smith from Supermarine and Kurt Tank, who had designed the Focke-Wulf 190, the main rival to the Spitfire, together with Witold Challier, who was Polish and Rolls-Royce's chief performance engineer for aircraft, for dinner at the Grosvenor House Hotel in London.

At first the atmosphere was chilly; here was the famous German designer from Prussia, vanquished but unbowed; the Polish emigré, bitter against the Germans; the two successful British designers, who were rivals anyway; and myself, quite neutral and hoping that from an engine point of view I might learn something! It was only six months or so since the war had ended; therefore, it was all very fresh in our minds. After two or three drinks before dinner, the atmosphere began to thaw out. We were able to converse in English since, fortunately, both Tank and Challier were bilingual.

After a few remarks about the shortcomings of one another's aircraft, their good points were accepted and doodles began to appear on the back of the menu, mostly, I may say, by Kurt Tank. Swept wings, the pros and cons, came under discussion; futuristic designs began to appear, peeps into the future on how rocket airliners would be able to cross the Atlantic in under an hour and so on.

The party became cordial and ended with Kurt Tank telling a story of how he was flying a Me 108 sport plane from France back to Germany when he was found by two Spitfires. They attacked him and shot off an aileron, causing him to force-land in a field. He then said, "Why did they not press home their attack and finish me off? Then there would not have been a Fock-Wulf 190 to fight against!" Then he said, "You should find out who the pilots were; they should be reprimanded!" Two years later he went to Argentina and designed the jet Pulqui, using a Rolls-Royce Derwent engine.

Kurt Tank's daughter, Ingrid, came over to England and lived with my family for several months to learn English and to help look after my two daughters. It seems almost inconceivable that all this could have happened so soon after the war and had I been told beforehand that this could come about, I would have been very skeptical. War is a crazy thing. One remembers that at the beginning of World War II, in 1939, the Russians were in treaty with the Germans; Britain was supported by France and after their defeat they fought against us; we fought against the Italians and then they were on our side; the Russians became our allies, and as soon as the Germans were beaten the Soviets once more became the potential enemy. There seems little point in it all, but it is remarkable that the defeated countries seem in some cases to have recovered more rapidly than the victors!

After I left Hucknall to go to London, things changed very much. At Hucknall there were fewer aeroplanes, since the RAF was being cut down; they were all jets, mostly Canberras, Hunters, Swifts and civil types. It was all becoming very costly and professional and perhaps more serious. The management, too, had changed; there were new pilots, many more technicians and ground equipment, including a wind tunnel. After Rolls-Royce's acquisition of the Bristol Company, which also had a flight test department but with a much superior aerodrome at Filton, the flying was transferred to Bristol, leaving Hucknall as a technical test department.

CHAPTER **12**

Postwar Motor Cars

WHEN World War II was over, the huge production of aero engines rapidly declined; it did, fortunately, receive a fillip since the RAF was to be reequipped with jets to replace the obsolescent piston engines. This meant employing new techniques and new machine tools, which kept the work force from dwindling away too rapidly. There was also a build-up of civil aviation, which kept the later types of piston engine still in production (turbines did not enter into the airlines until some years later with the advent of the Viscount and the Comet); but the massive production of the wartime air force was over.

Nevertheless, there was no going back to the prewar days when the Derby factory was large enough to cope with both motor cars and aero work. There was enough work on aero engines to keep not only Derby but Glasgow, too, occupied. It was decided to restart the motor car manufacture at the Crewe works.

At first it was not clear what the market might be for luxury motor cars; the country was economically impoverished, and a Labour government had been voted in with ministers impatient to force socialist ideologies on the taxpayer. This led to the accentuation of class distinction, a "them" and "us" complex, which made those lucky enough to own a fine car of quality feel embarrassment when visiting poorer areas where people were becoming unemployed and disgruntled. Not only this, but taxes had been raised out of all proportion, which made it necessary to earn unheard-of amounts in order to have sufficient left to buy an expensive car. All this made it almost essential that in order to obtain a Rolls or a Bentley, it had to be on the company books rather than be acquired as the property of an individual. This in itself may have turned out to be a good thing, not realized at the time, as it made the "best car" a status symbol. In effect, if a firm wished to be considered top class, the chairman and managing director would have to buy one of our cars. This was the general climate in which decisions had to be made regarding the future policy of the motor car division. The team of engineers previously employed on car design were reinstated from their wartime aero engine activities, the late prewar designs were put into production and selling commenced.

The motor car division became separate from the aero engine division, as also did the diesel engine activity. These latter were run by Dr. Llewelyn Smith as the managing director; he had joined the company from Oxford University around 1933 and had been in lodgings with me when I was working with Ray Dorey on the R engine test beds. Smith had done well as manager at the Glasgow factory during the war and was promoted to take over these two divisions. He was ably assisted by my old friend Ray Dorey as general manager; we had been each other's best man at our respective weddings and later he had been my boss at the Hucknall flight test department. The diesel engine division produced industrial diesel engines of a wide range of powers for marine launches, tractors, light locomotives, etc.

The motor car division at Crewe went into production with the Mark VI Bentley and Silver Dawn Rolls-Royce, and also made a few Wraith limousines. The postwar cars differed mainly from the earlier models by having what was basically the six-cylinder, 4½-liter engine which now had exhaust side valves and inlet overhead valves. An all-steel body designed and built by Rolls-Royce superceded the old coach-built ones, and independent front springing was also incorporated.

As mentioned, the market in Britain was hampered by certain restrictions imposed by the government; there was, however, a good demand from abroad. In America, the Bentley was not nearly so well known as the Rolls, so it was decided to fit a Rolls radiator on the Bentley and call it a Rolls-Royce Silver Dawn; this model was at first for export only and sold well.

The Silver Wraith was superceded by the Phantom IV, which was sold mainly for royalty and heads of state; it in turn was developed into the Phantom V so that this exclusive market was maintained. The Bentley Mark VI with minor improvements became the R type. This basic engine design, which had proved so successful, was now to be built for use in army and industrial vehicles in the form of four, six and eight cylinders.

In spite of the difficult conditions of trade both at home and abroad, production and sales increased, thus showing that the postwar formula had been sound: automatic gear boxes were introduced and, later than most cars, disc brakes became standard; engine power increased to keep pace with competitors but refinement was never neglected. I was very fortunate in being able to travel some quarter of a million miles in Bentley cars, since after I gave up flying I was allocated a Bentley, instead of a Spitfire, Hurricane or Mustang, to travel about in on my visits to the RAF and the various aircraft firms.

I was given my first Bentley shortly after I went to the London office. It was the custom of the company to allocate Bentleys to the directors for their general use, a very nice "perk" indeed. I was not a director, but a special case, like my predecessor, Bill Lappin, who, although never a director, used to travel around the aerodromes from early days in either a twenty-horsepower Rolls or a Bentley. I found that I, too, needed respectable transport, so I went up to Derby one day to see Lord Hives and suggested the company might be willing to go shares in a secondhand Bentley. He thought for a

minute and then said, "You don't want to buy a secondhand car."
He then picked up the telephone and spoke to Llewelyn Smith at
Glasgow and told him to send 8-B-5, one of the Mark V prototypes,
down to London, as it was wanted for another job—that was for me.
No wonder we were fond of the "old man"!

I used this car for six years and then one day, just before the
motor show, I received a cryptic note from the commercial director
which said, "Please contact Jack Scott and choose your color
scheme for a new Bentley which you have been allocated; your old
Bentley is urgently wanted for another job." This was a terrific thrill;
I was being treated like a cash customer, but just to take the gilt off
slightly, the bit about wanting the old one for another job was put
in. It was required to be broken up!

I ran the new R type (SLG-147) for eight years, doing close on
one hundred thousand miles, mostly in the British Isles, apart from
three tours in Europe to the South of France, and several trips to
Germany. The car went well throughout and never let me down.
When I handed it back in exchange for an R-type Continental, the
body work was also in very good condition. The Continental
Bentley then served me until the company went bankrupt and I left!
It also notched up around one hundred thousand miles with no
problems; everywhere we went it was much admired and this
included several trips to Germany where it was able to show a clean
pair of heels to most cars on the autobahns.

Being selected to supply the Royal Family with motor cars was a
notable achievement. For many years Daimler had been the
supplier. Daimler was an older company and well established as
makers of luxury cars. So, rather naturally, it became the make of
the royal car. It was up to Rolls-Royce to wrest the laurels away, not
an easy task, as one can imagine, in spite of being generally
acknowledged as the "Best Car in the World."

This change seemed to come about gradually through several
circumstances. In the early 1950s, before Princess Elizabeth
became queen, she and Prince Philip visited the Derby works; while
they were in the experimental department, Prince Philip's attention

was drawn to a straight eight-cylinder experimental Bentley car, nicknamed the "Scalded Cat" because of its brisk acceleration and smooth performance. He went for a test run which slightly delayed the proceedings and he was duly impressed; the suggestion was that when the car was fully developed they would be interested in having one but in the guise of a Rolls-Royce rather than a Bentley. Soon afterwards a Rolls-Royce Phantom IV using the eight-cylinder engine materialized, and was delivered to Princess Elizabeth and Prince Philip.

Shortly after this, Princess Elizabeth became queen and now there are five Rolls-Royce cars in the royal stables. There had been several Rolls cars owned by various members of the Royal Family for years; the Prince of Wales, who became Edward VIII for a short time, had had a Phantom II Continental Tourer in 1928. My brother and I delivered it, after repair, from Derby to Lilliehall. We did the journey in under two hours, early in the morning!

The reputation of Rolls-Royce as manufacturers of superlative, quiet cars has been jealously maintained against all comers—Mercedes, Daimler, Cadillac and Ford—and it still remains the "Best Car in the World." It is recognized as such and as a status symbol. If one has reached the pinnacle of success, whether a pop star or an industrial tycoon, the most eminent must own a Rolls-Royce car.

Her Majesty the Queen has now had a series of Rolls-Royce cars; her latest and a very special one, costing over eighty thousand pounds, was a Silver Jubilee gift from the Society of Motor Manufacturers and Traders. The president in 1978 happened to be David Plastow, the managing director of Rolls-Royce Motors Ltd.

Only recently I came across a Merlin-engined hybrid Rolls car; it was parked next door to a friend. I couldn't resist knocking at the door and asking if I could examine it since I was interested in Rolls cars! The owner was most helpful and we had an interesting chat about it. He was primarily interested in supplying automatic gearboxes and conceived the idea of putting a Merlin into a Silver Cloud chassis; this he carried out with considerable ingenuity by dispensing with the supercharger, turning the engine round back to front and coupling it through the gearbox to a strengthened propeller shaft and back axle. He built a neat sports saloon body and a long ten-foot hood under which was to be found the Merlin; altogether it looked most businesslike, with four large exhaust pipes protruding out the back. He told me it would do over two hundred miles per hour and I believed him. He showed me a standing start up the road that was really impressive; with a roar of the engine, clouds of black smoke from the exhausts, and burning rubber from the spinning wheels (which continued to spin for hundreds of yards), he disappeared into the distance.

I must say that when it started up, this hybrid was very noisy. One could hear the tappets and other mechanical noises, which aero engines invariably have since their clearances are fairly large compared with a motor car engine; under normal aero use, however, these noises are drowned out by the open exhaust. But the car had a slow tick-over and was docile in traffic; the owner had been pottering about in London traffic with no difficulty apart from blowing out smoke, due to rich slow running, with high oil consumption.

This man further told me that on two occasions, once in Germany on the autobahn and once on the M1 motor way, he was cruising along at about a hundred when he was overtaken by a Lamborgini; he quietly put his foot down until the Lamborgini was doing about 150 miles per hour and had not yet passed him. Then he opened up to 200 miles per hour and that was that. A similar thing had happened with a Ferrari in Germany! I told my friends at Rolls about this car, suggesting they should have a look at it—and to my surprise, I heard the sequel to these episodes. The owner of the Lamborgini, having noted the number of the Merlin Rolls, wrote to Crewe and said that a super experimental Rolls-Royce had left him standing and that when the car went into production could he have the first one! Unfortunately, the car caught fire and was destroyed, but I believe was later rebuilt.

This car proved rather an embarrassment to the company, as it carried the reputation of the company by virtue of its Rolls radiator. The company had not been consulted on its construction, so mechanically it was not approved in any way. Many of the chassis parts were of other companies' manufacture. The risk of legal proceedings was an ever-present worry; so, perhaps these ventures by enthusiasts, although of interest but built as a hotchpotch are rather a menace from a commercial company's point of view. Nevertheless, to the enthusiast and others interested in the unusual, they provide a rather welcome change from the orthodox.

CHAPTER 13

The Jet Age Arrives

I FIRST heard of gas turbines and jet propulsion while attending a research meeting chaired by Hives in the summer of 1941. Dr. Griffiths, our chief scientist at Rolls-Royce, produced a drawing and laid it on the table, proceeding to explain how his contra-flow gas turbine would work. It seemed to me to be very complex, rather difficult to understand and hardly practical, particularly at this stage of the war when we were only just beginning to get onto the offensive in a small way. We were under constant air attack at night and also being beaten back in the North African desert while the Germans were going through the Soviets like a warm knife through butter! I felt that all energies should be spent on improving what we had and that this complex device was rather irrelevant.

However, at this meeting Stanley Hooker got up and asked Hives whether he could be allowed to assist Air Commodore Whittle with his jet engine, which was in development under Air Ministry contract with Power Jets Ltd. They were having problems and had asked for some help. Hives immediately said, "Of course, by all means; we are all in this together."

At the next meeting I attended, several months later, active participation by Rolls-Royce in the Whittle engine project was discussed. The Griffiths concept had been relegated to low priority, and the Whittle jet was to be developed energetically. In fact, a complete department was set up to do this. A factory was procured at Barnoldswick in Yorkshire and Hooker was put in charge. He formed a design office with Adrian Lombard, a brilliant engineer from the Rover Car Company, as his chief assistant. An engine was fitted in the tail of a Wellington bomber as a flying test bed to be flown at Hucknall. The Rover Car Company had been selected by the Air Ministry originally to become involved with the Whittle engine. Hives, now realizing the great potential of this simple design, decided that only Rolls-Royce could do it justice. He persuaded the ministry and Rover that in exchange for taking over the Whittle engine development from Rover, Rolls-Royce would give them rights for the Merlin tank engines.

It was now realized that the Germans might be ahead in gas turbine development and that in the fairly near future there could be squadrons of German jets operational in the field. There was the Me 262 twin-jet fighter, the Arado twin-jet light bomber and the Me 163 rocket fighter all coming along; this gave impetus to the urgent need to develop a satisfactory and reliable jet engine.

The original Whittle engine, now named the Welland, was based on a centrifugal compressor with reverse flow to the turbines designed to give fifteen hundred pounds of thrust. At first only fourteen hundred pounds of thrust was produced but soon, under further development, a type test was passed in April 1943 at a figure of seventeen hundred pounds. The Gloster E.28/39 single-seat experimental aeroplane was fitted with a Welland that gave only twelve hundred pounds of thrust, but it flew well in the hands of Jerry Sayer and demonstrated that the principle was sound.

Gloster was asked to build an aeroplane to specification f.9/40 to be a twin-engine jet fighter, in which two Wellands would be installed. A production order was placed for both the airframe and the engine, and after further development they went into service in

616 Squadron. We did much of the test flying at Hucknall; it was an interesting experience flying jets for the first time. They had very slow acceleration since the thrust in those days was low, but once airborne the Meteor could show a clean pair of heels to any piston-engined fighter. We used to creep up slowly on a Mustang or Spitfire when out on test and maintain formation with them, noting the surprise on the pilot's face, then open the throttles and zoom away leaving them standing. Of course there was a "security clamp" on all jets and the average squadron pilot one encountered just didn't know what this strange bird was!

Meanwhile Hooker and Lombard had been exceedingly active on design and had produced the Derwent. This was an improvement on the Welland as it had straight-through combustion and gave two thousand pounds of thrust. This engine superceded the Welland in the Meteor and gave a much better performance. They were used in action, first chasing V-1 "flying bombs" with considerable ease, while the best piston-engined fighters even using plus twenty-five pounds of boost had quite a struggle to overtake them. The Derwent V, developed later, gave thirty-six hundred pounds thrust; and in the Meteor IV it took the World's Speed Record at 603 miles per hour in October 1945 and made 616 miles per hour the following year.

There was competition, encouraged by the Ministry of Supply which was supporting other turbine engine companies, as well as Rolls-Royce. The De Havilland engine company was developing the Goblin and the Ghost as engines for their own aeroplanes, the Vampire and the Venom, fighters which were competitors of the Meteor. These engines were generally similar to the Rolls-Royce design, except that they used the single-sided impeller, whereas Rolls followed Whittle in favoring the double-sided one. Both methods had certain advantages. In those early days when the technology of turbine engines was in its infancy there were many arguments both among the firms' engineers and in the services who used these engines. The single-sided impeller gave a better air-intake efficiency but was considerably larger in diameter.

When the war was over, the RAF squadrons were naturally run down; fortunately the advent of the jet had made the piston-engined fighters obsolete and so the remaining fighter squadrons were reequipped with Meteors and Vampires. There was also a need to encourage exports, both to reduce the redundancy in the factories and also to become established in as many foreign countries as possible. Many countries were embarking on a program of building up their own air forces again now that Germany had been beaten and there was a new threat from Russia.

My team of liaison test pilots consisted of Peter Birch, Harry Bailey, Rendell Stokes, Dick Peach, Tony Martindale and myself. We found ourselves with little to do now that the war was over and the Royal Navy and the Royal Air Force were being cut back. We did still have all the newly reequipped jet squadrons to visit and assist with the operation of this new type of engine, but we began to wonder what was in store for us.

Hives sent for me one day and said, "You are now going to form the 'Flying Squad' and go out into Europe to appoint agents and obtain orders to keep the factory going." This sounded exciting; he went on to say, "If they kick you down the stairs, don't give in; go up the back way!" This was about all the brief we were given! Harry Bailey was allotted France, Italy and Switzerland; Stokey took Turkey and the Middle East, and I decided to take on the Scandinavian and Low Countries.

I used our Percival Proctor to fly around in, taking Group Captain Tim Morice with me, as he was an old friend and sales representative for Dunlop. We went first to Holland. It was all very strange as the war had been over for only a short time; these once-occupied countries were struggling to get themselves organized again for peace. I found our prewar agent in a small restaurant with his bicycle chained to a lamppost outside; it had no tires fitted, because they were so scarce. It turned out that he was no longer suitable to be our agent because he had been too close to the Germans during the war. He was now *persona non grata!*

We moved on to Belgium and found François Vandegote, who

looked after us very well; he was well informed and knew everybody in the Belgian armed forces, convincing me that he was the right person to become our agent. As yet, however, the Belgian authorities were not ready to buy anything! The next stop was Copenhagen, where I was able to appoint Mogens Hartung. He, too, was very helpful, but again the Danes were not yet ready to order anything.

Norway was the next country on the list; here we were able to find our prewar agent and he was reappointed; again, we were too soon on the scene to sell anything. There was, however, hope for the future because these countries were shortly to be given some redundant Spitfires, Mustangs and Mosquitos so that they could build up their new air forces.

We then flew on to Sweden; here things were quite different since the Swedes had been neutral during the war. The country was opulent and the people well clothed and healthy looking, particularly the ladies, who were quite outstanding. The restaurants were attractive and the food was excellent. We were rather limited in what we could spend in that our overseas allowance was limited to 10 pounds per day.

The news soon got around that Rolls-Royce and Dunlop were looking for agents in Sweden. We had callers at our hotel from prospective applicants. There was a prince representing one firm of agents, and several well-known and well-connected firms came to see us; one even caught me in the bath! We were lavishly entertained, taken on board a yacht; it was all very pleasant after wartime austerity. I appointed a firm of agents but only if they would work for 1¼ percent; the Swedish government insisted upon this because De Havilland had just sold them some Vampires, which were expensive; the agent had received the usual 5 percent and the government had not liked this.

I also was delighted when our new Swedish agents gave me an order for two miles of phosphor-bronze strip, for putting onto skis! I had been so impressed by Hives's exhortations to obtain orders that this seemed rather good. On our arrival back to the works, he said,

"Goodness gracious, we aren't so hard up as all that." But we delivered the bronze strip anyway.

When I told Hives about appointing the Swedish agent and agreeing to the 1¼ percent commission, he said, "We can't have anybody working for us for that," and he sent a memo to Colonel Derby in London telling him to confirm a commission of 2½ percent. Colonel Derby then thought that 2½ percent was too little and wrote a letter awarding them 5 percent. Shortly afterwards an order was placed for a number of Avon engines and then a license; this added up to several million pounds and so our agents made a fortune, much to the annoyance of the Swedish government! This shows that we did not know very much about commerce at the time. The other members of the Flying Squad had similar experiences in their parishes. We used to visit these countries frequently building up goodwill and setting the scene for substantial orders that have increased as their armed forces have expanded. Civil aviation was also beginning to expand, but, because the Americans dominated the airline market with the DC-3, DC-4, DC-6 and the Lockheed Constellation, we did not break into this market until the coming of the Viscount.

We had some interesting and sometimes dangerous flights due to bad weather conditions and occasional lack of fuel. Sometimes we had to land in fields, and it was often more exciting than routine test flying. One day leaving Copenhagen in the Proctor to fly to Amsterdam, I somehow got my aircraft papers mixed up with those of Bill Pegg, who was flying a Bristol Freighter to Sweden. On arrival at our various destinations the customs officers couldn't understand how the descriptions of the aircraft were so different from the actual aeroplanes! We eventually got things sorted out after some delay and lots of international telephone calls!

Another day I flew back from Copenhagen against the wind, taking about eight hours to do the journey. On arrival at Hucknall, I buzzed my house to let my wife know that I was back. She arrived at the aerodrome in the car all dressed up in evening clothes and said, "Have you forgotten, we are going to a dance in the country?" I had to go home and get changed, then drive out into the country to the dance. I finally got to bed at 3:00 A.M.; quite a long day!

Gloster Aircraft Company and Rolls-Royce decided to mount a sales campaign in Europe as a joint venture. The timing was opportune as the World's Speed Record had just been taken by Eric Greenwood, Gloster's chief test pilot, and by Group Captain Willy Wilson. Both were flying Meteors. The two companies jointly funded the purchase of a Meteor and the expenses of the tour.

Digger Coates-Preedy was selected to demonstrate the Meteor while Eric Greenwood and I looked after the sales angle and flew the De Havilland Rapide carrying the luggage, spares and sales literature. We first visited Holland, then Denmark, Norway, and Sweden, and finally Belgium. It was not long before we found that De Havilland was doing the same thing and following us around. Dickie Blyth was flying the Vampire; he was an old friend from wartime days and so the competition was quite amicable but keen.

The highlight of this tour came when both teams arrived in Belgium at the same time; it was decided by the Belgian authorities to have a joint demonstration. The Meteor took off first, and all went well. Then an experienced Belgian pilot was invited to fly it. He was suitably briefed on what to do, but unfortunately he forgot to get his wheels up before he reached the limiting speed for wheels down! He then put on an impressive aerobatic performance with the nose wheel dangling in the air and one of the main wheels half out. When he landed, the undercarriage collapsed and he finished up on his belly along the runway. We were most perturbed and thought our chances of a sale would now be gone.

It was now the Vampire's turn and exactly the same thing occurred! Poor Dickie Blyth was now in the same predicament; the two aircraft were lying side by side on their bellies within yards of each other. After the tour, we reported to our various sales organizations what we thought the results were likely to be and which countries would buy Meteors and Vampires. We thought that we would win Holland and Denmark but were rather doubtful about Belgium. In fact, the Gloster Rolls-Royce team won all except Norway and Sweden. Export of Meteors to other countries went well, too, including sales to Argentina.

Back at Hucknall there was much activity in jet flying and installation development. The emphasis had shifted away from piston engines, except for the introduction of the Merlin into civil aviation, a new venture that was thought to have a bright future. The Lancaster bomber formed the basis of Britain's entry into the airline business. A version adapted to carry perhaps twenty passengers was named the Lancastrian. It was to be operated by Trans Canada Airlines (now renamed Air Canada) and by British South American Airways; another and more commodious version, the York, which carried sixty people, was operated by British Overseas Airways. All these variants used the Merlin 500 series engine.

The RAF Transport Command also operated the York. Much intensive sales effort was put in to compete with the United States on transport aircraft. The United States had the big advantage of converting to civil production before the war ended, using the Douglas DC-3 and DC-4 which were operating all round the world due to America's international involvement. Britain had been concentrating on building fighters and bombers and using American aircraft for transport. The Merlin, however, was able to penetrate into the DC-4 as a power plant and a number of them were built both for TCA and BOAC by Canadair, a subsidiary of General Dynamics in Montreal.

The lessons learned from these operations proved invaluable because of the exacting demands of the customer and the need for commercial experience and financial profit. This discipline was new and quite different from the prodigal way in which the RAF had been operating during the war. The Merlin made a name for itself based on reliability backed by good service; it was now able to use plus-twenty-five pounds of boost for takeoff and carrying passengers, a long cry from the beginning of the war when it was using only six pounds! This was Rolls-Royce's initiation into civil aviation to be followed later by an incursion into some of the major

American and Canadian airlines with the turbo-propeller engines and the bypass jets, followed later by the giant fan jets of the present vintage.

The Nene was the next Rolls-Royce engine to be built; it gave five thousand pounds of thrust and incorporated a double-entry impeller which allowed for a much smaller-diameter engine. It was very successful. When the Nene jet engine was under development, it first flew in the Lancastrian test bed, being installed in the two outboard positions while the two Merlins were retained in the inboard positions. The first application to a fighter was in the Vampire. It was thought that the five thousand-pound thrust engine would give a marked improvement in performance over the De Havilland Goblin of thirty-five hundred pounds of thrust; it certainly did better on takeoff and climb, but was only about the same speed in level flight. It was discovered that this was because of the inefficiency of the air intake, due to the double-sided impeller at high speed. In spite of this, the French ordered Nenes and the Australians bought them, too. The U.S. Air Force sent a Lockheed Shooting Star to Hucknall to have a Nene fitted. This was accomplished in six weeks and produced a first-class result, much superior to the Allison engine previously fitted. So the USAF bought a large quantity and so did the Canadians.

Since development work had been proceeding in Britain, much information had been passed on to America, where progress had not been so rapid. In order to catch up, licenses were taken to manufacture several of the British engines. Pratt and Whitney bought the Nene license and the later model of the Tay so that they could produce engines for the Lockheed Shooting Star and Grumman Panther. The Panther was the result of a U.S. Navy study and was able to be built only because the Nene engine could be used. At first, the U.S. Navy resisted because the engine was British and it was policy not to rely on a foreign engine. This problem was overcome when Pratt and Whitney went into licensed production of the engine then being called the J-48; a later model, the Tay, gave sixty-five hundred pounds of thrust; this was also built by Pratt and Whitney and was used in the Grumman Cougar, a development of the Panther. The Canadians also built these engines in a factory at Montreal run by Rolls-Royce of Canada.

Both the Nene and the Tay were licensed to France and were built by Hispano-Suiza in Paris. These engines were used by the French to power all their prototype jet aircraft, the most successful of which was the Dassault Ouragon later to be followed by the Mystère.

Just about this time, the British Socialist Minister of Economic Affairs, Sir Stafford Cripps, instructed Rolls-Royce to sell a quantity of Nene and Derwent engines to the Soviets! The company was not keen to do this and would not allow the Soviet representatives inside the factory while the engines were being built; nor would they allow them to have details of the starter panel. They consoled themselves that the Russians would not be able to copy the engine as they would not be able to reproduce the sophisticated materials for the turbine blades and other intricate parts, since they were not granted a manufacturing license. But the Soviets astounded everybody by copying these engines and putting them into production quite quickly, engining their MIG-15s and MIG-17s with them and using them against the United States in the Korean war.

Now that jet aeroplanes were exceeding 650 miles per hour it was realized that the centrifugal compressor engine with its large diameter was to be a limiting factor for higher speeds, particularly when supersonic speeds would shortly be desired. Design work had been proceeding on axial flow compressors which would greatly reduce the diameter of the engine and also permit higher compression ratios, thereby improving the fuel consumption. Not very much was known about these axial flow compressors and their behavior, so development was not so rapid as with the centrifugal type; the cost of development, too, was to be much more costly. The Rolls-Royce Avon was the first axial flow engine from the stable, its competitor being the Armstrong-Siddeley Sapphire.

CHAPTER 14

Jet Trainers

THE transition from piston-engined aircraft to jets meant that there had to be a rethinking in training circles as to the best method of training pilots. The general operation of a jet aeroplane is very different from that of a piston-engined aeroplane, not only from the flying aspect but in the engine handling methods for obtaining maximum performance. A jet aeroplane is much easier to fly in many ways, particularly during takeoff and landing. Piston-engined aeroplanes require greater changes of trim and sometimes rather violent manipulation of the controls to counteract engine torque and the plane's tendency to swing, due to the propeller slipstream. For maximum economy, a piston engine should run at full throttle with the revolutions per minute trimmed back to give the desired speed; altitude is of little importance. With a jet, the higher the altitude chosen, the better, for this enables the engine to run at high revolutions per minute, where it is most efficient. Due to the much higher speed and also higher fuel consumption of a jet, things happen much more quickly and one can get lost more easily; of course, the time available to rectify error also is much shorter, so that accuracy of navigation is of great importance with jets.

The thinking of the Air Ministry training branch at this time was not to my mind logical in that, they drew up a specification for a propeller turbine trainer based on the Rolls-Royce Dart engine. This did nothing for the pilot, for it presented the difficulties of flying a piston-engined propeller aircraft and offered no experience with a jet's high-speed, high-altitude flying in a pressure cabin.

Tony Martindale, one of my colleagues, and I decided to write a paper advocating a pure jet trainer and we roughed out a specification which would meet what we considered to be the requirements. We also believed that if we could initiate the design around a Derwent engine and persuade a suitable firm to build it, then Rolls-Royce would sell a lot of engines. We realized that De Havilland was very experienced in building trainers, and they also built the Goblin engine. So if they tumbled to it, they could jump the gun and beat us to it! There was also the problem that Rolls-Royce could do well commercially with the Dart turbo-propeller engine, in either of the official, government-selected firms' proposals. Since Avro and Boulton Paul Aircraft were invited to meet the official specifications, we were up against official government policy and Rolls-Royce policy; yet we knew that De Havilland was sitting in a good position if official policy swung towards a pure jet trainer. What should we do?

I explained the situation to Ray Dorey and Hives; Dorey agreed to get his installation engineers under Tom Kerry to do a layout of an aeroplane to meet our proposals, based on a Derwent. Hives said, "Be very careful not to upset the present policy, but keep up the study."

I decided to go to Holland to discuss the project with Fokker; they were looking for new projects on which to build up their company following the German occupation; also the Dutch Air Force was in the market for jet fighters, so Holland seemed to be the place to launch our jet trainer ideas. Piet Voss, the managing director of

Fokker, as well as Mr. Baling, the chief designer, and Van Meerten, his assistant, liked our idea and so did Professor Van der Maas of the Dutch government aircraft laboratory. They agreed to do a detailed design of a jet trainer using the Derwent engine and to build it for the Dutch Air Force. So far so good, but we told them it would have to be done in a hurry before De Havilland came in on the act!

In the meantime, the British Air Ministry decided to abandon the turbo-propeller trainer, but Avro and Boulton Paul Aircraft had already built their prototypes. These were to be re-engined with the piston-engined Merlin. This meant good steady business for Rolls, but to me it seemed a retrograde step. I had also been having conversations with Fred Miles of Miles Aircraft, builders of trainer aircraft, hoping they might design a jet trainer and then go to the Air Ministry and get it supported. I had even persuaded Hives to meet me there and talk about a joint project. Miles wanted Hives to take a stake in his equity but Hives would not accept. Rolls had once held 25 percent of that company many years before at the time of the building of the Kestrel, and it had not been a success; the other aircraft companies objected because they felt Rolls might pass on some of their ideas to a rival company. (There had been an amusing incident over this when Sir Arthur Sidgreaves, who was then the Rolls managing director, and Hives as head of the Rolls-Royce experimental department were visiting Fairey Aviation Company. Sir Richard Fairey had remarked to Hives and Sidgreaves, "We don't like your being involved with an aircraft company." It was at this time that Fairey was trying to start up an engine factory. So Hives replied, "We treat them just like we treat your engine." Fairey answered and asked, "How is that?" Hives replied, "As a bloody joke.") After that, it was realized that it was better to specialize in engines 100 percent and treat all aircraft companies equally. The other engine companies were associated with aircraft companies, but they never had Rolls-Royce's success in being selected to power the aircraft built by pure aircraft companies that were unaligned.

After the visit at Miles Aircraft, I rode back with Hives to Derby in his eight-cylinder experimental Rolls, but try as I could, I was unable to persuade him to support the Miles trainer, apart from being willing to lend them an engine. A week or so later just before the ministry gave the order to proceed with the Merlin trainer, Hives had to go to America. While he was waiting at London Airport to embark, he wrote me the following note: "We have decided to back the Merlin trainer. I want to make sure we do not find two sections competing with each other. We also have no interest in aircraft design. This is not to discourage you, but hold your horses until the Merlin trainer is decided." I think this shows rather well the broad thinking and understanding of Hives's willingness to let one get on with the job in one's own way.

Eventually, Boulton Paul Aircraft was awarded the contract and built the Balliol which had the Merlin fitted. Fokker Aircraft meanwhile was building a prototype called the S-14; they were also building a twin piston-engined trainer to a contract for the Dutch Air Force. They were not in a position to do both jobs with equal urgency and the twin was given priority; this was unfortunate, as the S-14 was delayed somewhat.

De Havilland at last saw the opportunity of getting into the market by building a side-by-side version of the Vampire as a jet trainer; so what we feared all along did happen. De Havilland's plane was ordered by the Air Ministry and became the standard jet trainer for the RAF and also was sold abroad in large quantities. The S-14 was completed and flew well but it was almost a year late. It was eventually ordered by the Dutch Air Force, the Derwent being replaced by the Nene to give it more power. Sonderman, the test pilot, took it over to America where it aroused much interest; the U.S. Air Force by now was considering going over to jets for training. I was told later that had it been available a year earlier the USAF would most likely have bought it and built it under license.

I look back on these days of advocating the jet trainer with pleasure; it was an interesting exercise, although only partially successful. It gave me experience at a time when the industry and the air forces were becoming reestablished after the war. I had the opportunity of meeting the up-and-coming young engineers in the various firms and making good friends while traveling to interesting places. In spite of my tending not to be in agreement with official policy, I felt that I was being permitted to use my own initiative. Hives, of course, knew what everyone was up to and he would check you if you were going too far astray. On one occasion during this time when I was becoming rather a bore about the jet trainer to the exclusion of other projects, he told me to ease up a bit and not to get "too closely associated with any one aeroplane or engine, as one gets typecast." Of course, he was right; but I always found if one did not go "flat out regardless," the many hurdles one had to overcome both at the works and with the Air Ministry would eventually get one bogged down, while the project one was pursuing would sink into the sand and disappear.

Lord Hives was always very broadminded and encouraged us to make friends with the customer; thus, a rapport was established which produced a mutual trust. In this way we were given genuine information on what the customer's requirements were and what should be done to improve the engines to suit any particular environment. It was considered of great importance that we not be suspected of "selling," just to get orders for engines. Some firms put salesmanship above the desire to give the customer what he really needed, but this was never the Rolls-Royce way. Rather, the opposite was the case and there were instances of advising the customer to go elsewhere if he would get something more suitable. In this way his confidence for the future was assured.

One instance of this was when an American aircraft company heard about a new model of Avon and indicated that they wished to place an order for it. They were told by Lord Hives that the engine was not ready but that, if they would like to wait for a year until development was completed, they could have it with pleasure.

Furthermore, great store was put upon rectifying troubles and investigating complaints at an early stage; no effort was spared in doing this. It paid off in the long run, as an epidemic of troubles could be stopped before they filtered through official channels with the usual delays and the danger of the company's reputation becoming tarnished.

All of this sprang from Hives's strong leadership and excellence of character. Roger Lewis, a good friend of ours and an American of high renown, having held several important positions in the Pentagon, Pan Am, General Dynamics and Amtrak, put it this way: "Rolls-Royce and Lord Hives were complementary to each other. Rolls-Royce would not have developed as it did had not Hives been in charge, and Hives would not have reached his stature without Rolls-Royce." This could well be true, as the character of Hives was so compatible with the principles of Rolls-Royce.

Hives always cared for the Rolls-Royce personnel and backed them up when necessary. On one occasion I decided to take an opportunity to go fishing in Scotland on the River Tweed, one of the most famous salmon rivers. Apart from the pleasure of fishing, my colleague Gordon Strangeways and I invited two important civil servants to join us; the boss agreed we could go and said, "Bring me back a salmon." I drove one of our guests up from London in my new Bentley, which I had only recently been given to replace the old Mark V I had used for many years.

Gordon and the other guest were due to arrive later by air. We thought this guest might like to drive the Bentley back to the hotel from the airport, but this was a bad mistake. He duly accepted the offer, remarking that he was not very experienced, having only driven a Morris Minor before. The road was wet and a little slippery so that when he came to a sharp corner, alas, he went straight on through the fence into a field, knocking off the exhaust pipe and damaging the front fender. Soon the farmer appeared and demanded compensation. Our guest was worried, fearing publicity and the possiblity of being accused of accepting hospitality from a contracting firm. However, we drove the car out of the field. I must say I wasn't very pleased by the damage done to my new Bentley, and with the exhaust sounding like an aero engine we reached the hotel rather late for dinner.

The next day we drove through the castle grounds to the riverside, the car still making noises like an aero engine. It was, to say the least, embarrassing! The fishing was excellent and the salmon cooperative, so by the time we packed up and went back to the hotel for dinner, we had caught eleven fish.

The next day was the same, another eleven fish; these were really going to be days to remember. About tea time, the duchess came down to meet us and when I had made myself know to her and she asked where our American guests were. I told her that there were no Americans but that we had two distinguished English guests with us; she seemed surprised and said, "But I thought they were Americans." With that she wandered away back to the castle. Gordon and I felt a little uneasy that there might be some misunderstanding somewhere, but decided not to worry; we would all go back to the hotel and have dinner, discuss our exploits and prepare for departure the next day, having had the Bentley exhaust pipe temporarily welded up.

On Monday, Gordon and I arrived at the Derby works and distributed the salmon amongst the Rolls-Royce directors, two for Lord Hives and the remaining ones for our guests and ourselves, which we put into deep freeze. We found Lord Hives's secretary waiting for us on the doorstep. She said, "He wants to see you." We went into his office and were greeted with "Hello, you bloody poachers, read this letter from the duke." It was a strong letter saying that two Rolls officials had gone fishing under false pretenses at a special low rental because there were to be two important American guests—so he was given to understand. He said that we had sold the fish and because it was the best time of the year, he would normally have been fishing the river himself. He had ordered drinks at the castle, which he had cancelled when he heard that there were no Americans present. Would Lord Hives take disciplinary action and deal with us in the appropriate manner!

We were a little taken aback, wondering how this misunderstanding had come about. Lord Hives said, "What did you do wrong?" We explained that, of course, we had not sold any fish. He smiled and remarked that he realized that and he was looking forward to eating his. He listened to our explanation that what probably had happened was that the agent, who had done the negotiations for us with the duke's estate office, had exaggerated about who our guests were in order to obtain this very exclusive fishing spot; this we were able to confirm later. Lord Hives said, "Take the letter, reply to it for me and I will sign it." This we did, pointing out that His Grace was entirely misinformed, that if he wanted a higher rental he could have it and that no fish had been sold; also that we had had a very successful and happy time.

This reaction to an awkward situation was typical of our chairman; we could always rely on him for help in trouble! Throughout his career there were many instances of this sort of human approach to controversial and difficult situations. Those two civil servants, as time went by, rose to the top of their profession, obtaining high honors; ever afterwards, when we had to transact business with them, this story would crop up, easing the tension and causing a smile. This sort of association with people always pays off in the long run; it is a matter of mutual confidence and camaraderie.

CHAPTER 15

A Peerage for Hs

Everybody in the company was delighted when we heard the news that Hives had been elevated to the peerage. It came through on June 16, 1950. Previously he had been awarded the Companion of Honour, a unique honor for an engineer which only a very limited number of people can hold at the same time. Hives had been offered a knighthood during the war for his outstanding work, but he had refused it, saying, "Let the people fighting the war have the honors; they deserve them; we are only doing our job." Now we felt that his great contribution in producing the "tools" which helped to win the war and in advancing engineering and technology in the international field—all of which reflected well on Great Britain—had been suitably rewarded.

A celebration to commemorate this event took the form of a luncheon in the works staff canteen. Representatives from all departments were invited. It was a friendly gathering, as many of the staff and works people had known each other for years and we all felt proud and had such great affection for the boss. The speeches were all from the heart and can describe better than I the sentiment which was felt at all levels. I shall quote from them as they sum up most lucidly the driving force and spirit which motivated the company and which had been continually sustained by the personality and leadership of Lord Hives.

Having received the honor, Hives sent a message to the workers which read: "It is my wish that the great honor which has been conferred upon me by His Majesty should be shared by all Rolls-Royce workers."

After lunch Mr. Harry Swift, the general works manager, who had been with the company for many years, spoke first and said: "We are here to celebrate the elevation of Mr. Hives to the peerage, an honor well merited and long overdue. It is a great occasion for the company, the town, the industry and his friends and colleagues, and sets the seal on a distinguished career. During the forty years I have known Hs, he has always been in the forefront of Rolls-Royce achievements. Even in the early days of this factory, Hs as a tester was always striving for quieter cars and I as a charge hand-fitter on axles was always doing my best to please him.

"Later in life another of his achievements was the London/ Edinburgh trial which ended with a speed test on the Brooklands track of one hundred miles per hour with a standard car already world famous. In those days he was chief of a very small experimental department, directly under the control of the late Sir Henry Royce.

"In the 1914–18 war Hs was responsible for the development of the Rolls-Royce aero engines, Eagle, Falcon, and Hawk. For these and other outstanding services during the war, he was awarded the Member of Order of the British Empire. Later came the Atlantic crossing in 1919 by the Vickers Vimy with Eagle engines; he had a finger in this pie too; then came the well known success on the Schneider Trophy races. He was also busy with motor development. The Silver Ghost went. The Phantom and Wraith were born. Subsequently, the Rolls-Bentley when the Bentley company was taken over by Rolls-Royce.

"Now during the idle periods, the Kestrel aero engine was

designed and developed and this engine put into production on then modern lines. The next serious and important stage was when the Nazi war clouds began to gather. Rolls-Royce was asked to tackle an expansion program of large, modern and efficient aero engines, and it was Hives who shouldered the responsibility of developing the Merlin, which as is only too well know engined the Spitfires and Hurricanes, Lancasters, Mosquitos, Mustangs, etc., which put us on the right road to victory; otherwise this honor celebration might never have taken place at all.

"Just about this time, advancement again followed on the heel of achievement, and Hs in 1936 succeeded the late Arthur Wormald as general works manager, and it was under his personal example and leadership that Rolls-Royce, by common assent, became, as far as aero engines were concerned, the principle factor in the winning of the second Great War. During this period, Hs was offered a knighthood, but refused such an honor whilst Britain was striving to live and might go under.

"After final victory was assured, Hs was made a Companion of Honour, a magnificent acknowledgment of his personal achievements and leadership in the field of aeronautical engineering.

"When he joined the company in 1908, it was an era in which men accepted inequality of opportunity as a challenge—a challenge to be met by enterprise and resource and Hs met it in the fashion we know so well, hard work and honest endeavor. Never have I met a man who liked work so much; we all remember his battle cry, 'Work till it hurts'; another one, 'Work is the best fun on earth providing there is no bitterness and no financial grabbing.'

"There have been other outstanding personalities over the years I have been associated with Rolls-Royce, but surely none greater than Hs. Great because he had the strength of character and an indomitable purpose to work for an ideal, well exemplified in the 'Magic of the Name'; and it is in keeping with such a man that so many of his old colleagues and men long in the service of the company are here today. They have all helped, however humble their task. I don't think anyone, workers or government, ever doubted that we, as a team, would do our share in the fight and that we would do more than keep pace with the enemy.

"This teamwork was an outstanding tribute to his fine quality of leadership and to his tremendous breadth of vision. The Royal Air Force got the engines in the quantities and quality they wanted. The success of our first efforts was assured by the unselfish devotion to their duty of the company's servants, none more so than Hs who, despite his claim to be 'only a mechanic,' did nevertheless set an example and a tempo in the true sense of the word. His was the responsibility not only to provide the quantities, but to see that quality remained the watchword, and this honor is a vote of confidence from our fighting units, the RAF and others. He had the courage and ability to stick to an ideal under the greatest stress and to navigate this organization despite its temporary vast and unwieldy expansion, strictly in accordance with traditions proven in peacetime and indispensable in war.

"Never has an award of His Majesty been so richly deserved and seldom has it been received with greater modesty and humility.

"To those who will have to continue this policy and tradition, I say he has laid a fine foundation for the future and this responsibility must be accepted when the time comes for him to relinquish the reins."

Lord Hives then replied:

"I cannot begin to tell you how much I appreciate you all giving up your time to come here today.

"I know you all know that the honor which has been conferred on me is a national recognition to the Rolls-Royce Company, and the company includes all the workers, past and present, and especially includes people who are here today, because I can see around me the people who have given of their best to build up our reputation.

"I have been deeply touched by the little notes of congratulation and praise which I have received from all sections. The messages I have received confirm that we are a very happy organization.

"You have often heard me say that I consider work to be the best fun on earth, and working for Rolls-Royce is even better.

"I think, considering our numbers and considering how we are separated by long distances, that there is a wonderful spirit of pride and loyalty, and we do not suffer from cliques or factions. To me, that is something we must always cherish and maintain.

"I can remember the time in the Derby works when everybody walked about in fear and trembling of the [company] secretary! The accountants were looked upon as something unclean, and if you wanted to know the cost of a part in the Derby works the only fellow who could tell you was somebody sitting in an office in London. We have improved since then! You will find the accountants are quite human. The proof of that is that they can even make mistakes, and—better still—you can get them to admit it.

"There was a time when the directors sat in solemn conclave and held their meetings in London. On the rare occasions when they visited Derby, meetings were held in the Midland Hotel. It has now been agreed that London is a relatively unimportant place compared with either Derby, Crewe, or Glasgow.

"We are fortunate in our shareholders. We must never overlook the fact that the company belongs to the shareholders. If enough of them got together they could undoubtedly give me the sack! But as the shares are so widely held there is no cause for alarm. When they talk of the freezing of wages, Rolls-Royce dividends to the shareholders have been frozen for eleven years.

"When we rejoice at the success of the company at the present time, we must never overlook that it has only been made possible by the magnificent work of the people who laid down the ideals and built up the tradition of Rolls-Royce. In these we include Sir Henry Royce, Claude Johnson, Basil Johnson, Arthur Wormald and Sir Arthur Sidgreaves.

"It has been my policy faithfully to follow the ideals which were maintained by the founders of this great firm. It is difficult to go wrong on the engineering and technical side if we follow the policy laid down by Sir Henry.

"I would like to acknowledge the kindly cooperation we have

always received from the workers in the unions. I often boast to my friends that Rolls-Royce was one of the first companies in the country to recognize shop stewards and to make use of a full time convener. I certainly think we hold one record and that was an incident during the war when the shop stewards and the management on one side argued a case on women's wages against both the Employers' Federation and the Union Executives plus the Ministry of Labour. Needless to say, we won the point!

"One of the great changes in our business since the end of the War is the extension into foreign markets. There are few countries which are not our customers now. We have not only created new markets for our products but we have created new friends. In all parts of the world where our engines are either being manufactured under license or are being used, we have established a wonderful relationship. Personally, I place tremendous value on making your customers into your friends. One of the points which impressed me on my trips abroad was the appreciation there was for the moral business standard of the Rolls-Royce company; we must never allow a question of profit to jeopardize this position.

"Many people have remarked that the Honour is greatly overdue. I do not think I am giving any secrets away when I say that I was pressed to accept a title in the early days of the war, and later, but I was a conscientious objector to accepting any honor which was available to the men in the forces who were making great personal sacrifices. It was because of my objections that I was awarded the Companion of Honour which came within my specification, because it was not awarded to the services. It is generally given to the Church, to poets and men of letters, with, of course, Churchill and Atlee. I used to boast that I was the only 'plumber' in the Union but this was disputed by Mr. Essington Lewis the chairman of the Broken Hill Proprieties [BHP] Company in Australia who was awarded it the same year as myself and was a brother plumber!

"I have had numerous enquiries as regards what title I am going to adopt. The decision is a simple one; it will be the Rt. Hon. Lord

Hives of Duffield, in the County of Derby. Possessing no estates or lands, I see no justification for making things difficult by changing my name.

"It is my intention to maintain this Honour with respect and dignity, because I look upon it as a trust earned by all the grand people who have built up this company."

Certain compelling references in these two speeches merit serious thought: would many men refuse a knighthood today if it were offered or rather than wait until the job has been completed? But Lord Hives, being a humble man and in the true teaching of the Bible, did so, reaping his reward which he accepted not for himself, but on behalf of his work-mates and colleagues. This is truly the spirit of greatness.

Finally, there are some words from Sir George Edwards, O.M., who rose from the drawing office at Vickers to head up the British Aircraft Corporation as chairman and managing director. He has been responsible for many important projects including the Valiant bomber, the Vickers Viking, Vanguard, VC-10, BAC-111 and Concorde. His comments on Hives indicate that Hs was widely regarded virtually everywhere.

"Although I knew of and occasionally met the great man at Rolls-Royce, I really got to know Mr. Hives, as he then was, from September 1945, when I was appointed chief designer at Vickers-Armstrongs at Weybridge.

"During the war when I was experimental manager at Weybridge, I had fitted high altitude Merlin X engines into a stratospheric bomber based on the Wellington (never used in anger); there were a number of test-bed Wellingtons with jet engines in the tail and one with Dart engines as the only source of power, but the bulk of Weybridge engines came from Bristol.

"The Viscount was scheduled for a propeller turbine—the competing engines being the Rolls-Royce Dart and the Armstrong-Siddeley Mamba. The Dart had a centrifugal compressor and the Mamba had an axial type which, by virtue of the low rating (one thousand horsepower) was pretty small and to my mind fragile. A decision had to be made and when the time had come to do so, the choice was difficult. The prototype Mambas were doing well and running at pretty well the performance and weight specifications. The Dart on the other hand was underpower, overweight and up on fuel consumption.

"I knew that the wrong decision could set back turbine civil transports for years and a serious talk with Rolls, led by Hives, was called for. He brushed the inevitable cigarette ash off his ample waistcoat and said, 'It seems that we have some work to do.' I waved my arms about to make him understand just how much work, and the decision was taken to put their heads down and do it, rather than give it all up for a bad job. The result is history—hundreds of Viscounts—thousands of Darts in a variety of aeroplanes. There followed Avons in Valiants; Tynes in Vanguards; Conways in VC-10s; Speys in BAC-111s; Adours in Jaguars, and so on.

"Hives's bigness was shown up when the initial Avon compressor was in trouble. He promptly took his team to the Armstrong-Siddeley company to learn from their experience with the more docile Sapphire compressor.

"Hives had this strange process of calling everyone by initials. He was Hs to all the world. The whole outfit was run by symbols, such as Lom., Rbr. E, Psn., and so on. He held large meetings when there was trouble. His own staff used to tell him straight when he was on the wrong tack; and he liked it; but he was the boss.

"Most great pronouncements were something like this—a large pile of ash brushed off the long-suffering waistcoat, then, 'I see—(pause), Well, we'd better do this'—repeated—End. And what counted was that you knew it would be done.

"Unlike the Duke of Plaza Toro, Hives led his regiment very much from the front. 'Work until it hurts' was the battle cry. He had enormous reserves of physical and mental strength and drove himself relentlessly. His talented team (and let there be no doubt they knew their job) were so devoted to him that they drove themselves as hard; sometimes, because they lacked his strength, with damage to their own health.

"I have had the luck to work for, and with, some great people, and no one was kinder to me than Hs. He used to sit and explain the situation, operational, political, technical, with great patience and clarity. I grew very fond of him and really sat at his feet. I think he enjoyed the military/government part of the business more than the civil. He was first an engineer. He knew that in a high quality engineering concern if the engineering was not right, nothing else could save it. He was an engineer cast in the Brunel mold, and was as big a man. One of the greatest compliments I ever had as a younger man was when he chaired my inaugural lecture on my induction as president of the Royal Aeronautical Society.

"The nicest thing that happened was on June 16, 1950, when I went to Derby for a battle about something. I arrived in time for lunch around that famous circular table in Nightingale Road, to find champagne out and no visitors. The Honours List, which I had not seen, had that day announced his Barony. I protested to Ray Dorey that I should depart forthwith and not intrude on what was a family affair. Not so, said Dorey; Hs knew I was coming, and reckoned that by now I was as much part of the outfit as the others. 'Don't think I'm going to change or go soft,' Hs said (not that anyone in their right mind would). 'I'm still Hs and I'm going to go on being him.'

"Lord Hives of Duffield was a great engineer and a great man who served his country well and was respected and loved by all those who worked with him.

"Another great Englishman, Sir Francis Drake, had he known Hives, might well have had him in mind when he once said:

There must be a beginning of any great matter
But the continuing unto the end until it be thoroughly finished
Yields the true glory

"Hives found the true glory all right."

CHAPTER 16

The Jet Age Has Arrived

ROLLS-ROYCE, having well and truly become committed to building jet engines, was already leading the field in the late forties. Manufacturing licenses had been granted to the United States, France, Sweden, Belgium and Australia; the main competition came from Armstrong-Siddeley who was producing the Sapphire under contract from the British Ministry of Supply. This was an axial engine of similar specification to the Avon, both of which started life at six thousand pounds of thrust. There was little to choose between them; in fact, the Sapphire had a less sensitive compressor, an advantage, for the engine was less prone to surging when the guns were fired. This problem was later overcome and the developed Avon replaced the Sapphire in the Hawker Hunter and perhaps more notably in the supersonic Lightning. The Avon was the first engine to fly at supersonic speed when the Fairey Delta raised the World's Speed Record to 1,132 miles per hour on March 10, 1956.

The engine companies in the United States were making rapid progress in the design and development of gas turbines (jet) engines under the spur of the Korean War. The General Electric J-47, which powered the North American F-86 Sabre, was the mainstay of the fighter threat to the Soviets who were, alas, using the Russian copied version of the Rolls-Royce Nene in their MIG-15 and MIG-17 fighters. This caused much bitter feeling in the United States, quite rightly and the blame must go squarely on the shoulders of British Labour politicians who enforced the original sale of the engines to the Soviets. It was undoubtedly a grave blunder and one of several which I propose to reveal. The F-86 proved to be a very fine aircraft and many of them were built; the version built in Australia had Avon engines and due to its greater thrust gave a very good performance.

My test-flying days were drawing to a close when I was posted to the London office to become export sales manager and liaison representative with the military services and the aircraft industry, to succeed Bill Lappin. The main purpose of this job was to search out opportunities for Rolls-Royce engines to be selected for new aircraft and/or re-engineering of proven types which might be improved thereby. This assignment enabled me to travel worldwide and to study the general military market.

Rolls-Royce was at this time clearly the leader in the design of gas turbine engines; there were more types of aircraft using Rolls-Royce engines than any other manufacturer and more variations of the turbine engine had been designed and built, such as, pure jet, bypass (turbofan) jet, turbopropeller, centrifugal compressor and axial.

The development of the gas turbine and the aircraft to use them was moving apace under the influence of competition to equip the world market and to keep ahead of the Soviets. My "parish" which had to be visited included some nineteen independent British companies building aircraft; ten in Europe and all military-contracted firms in the United States (about another ten), plus Canada and Australia. Close contact had to be kept with the air staffs, who formulated the future requirements, and also, to a lesser extent, the naval staffs. This kept me pretty busy.

It was interesting being in a position to compare the way the different companies operated and how their general philosophies varied. Some of them were steeped in old traditions and were still controlled by their founders, for example, Sir Frederick Handley-Page, Sir Geoffrey De Havilland, Sir Roy Dobson of Avro, Marcel Dassault, Roy Grumman. Others had been fairly recently formed, such as English Electric and the emerging nationalized and state-owned conglomerations. Their motivation and progressiveness in looking to the future was often a factor to be taken into account when recommending their design proposals to the executives of Rolls-Royce. One was always, through past experience, careful about selecting good projects from reliable firms of high reputation, with a special eye on safety and good flying qualities. The reputation of an engine can be ruined by being married to an inferior aeroplane, as we had found out on several occasions. These recommendations needed careful judgment, as progress in aerodynamics was rapid and thus caused many unorthodox designs to be produced.

The reputation of the individual designers and the likelihood of their advanced projects becoming practicable and acceptable to the operators in the services had to be assessed. Often there was disagreement back at Derby as to which firm or project should be supported. Some of the younger, brilliant and up-and-coming engineers tended to favor designs of the firms who employed people of similar age groups and enthusiasm for new technology.

There was keen competition amongst the various aircraft firms designing fighter aircraft at this time. The Meteor and the Vampire had up to now been the chosen types to re-equip the RAF in transition from piston-engined aircraft to jets. Now in 1952, new designs were emerging employing more advanced aerodynamics such as swept-wings, axial flow engines with afterburners, etc.

From an engine-maker's point of view, I thought it would be of value if we could arrange discussions with the Central Fighter Establishment where the study of fighter tactics and requirements took place. CFE, as it was known, was the logical development of the old AFDU (Air Fighter Development Unit) which the reader will remember from when the Merlin Mustang was described. All new fighters came to CFE for evaluation as operational aircraft, having already been at Boscombe Down for aerodynamic and airworthiness tests.

I talked over the idea of having a test pilots' convention with Eric Greenwood, Gloster's chief test pilot and John Cunningham, the chief test pilot at De Havilland. They both agreed it was a good idea and so we approached the commandant of CFE, my good friend Paddy Crisham, and Fred Rosier, his chief of staff. They both concurred and so the first test pilots' convention took place.

We gathered a representative team from the industry: John Derry, Mike Lithgow, Rolly Beamont, Bob Tuck, Dave Morgan, Neville Duke and Wimpey Wade. The idea was that each should be quite open about experiences during development flying. The experts from the RAF would then give their opinions on how they felt the aircraft could be made more operational. Afterwards, we stayed the night and had a party at which everybody got to know one another pretty well. It was considered a great success and so it was decided to hold these meetings twice per year. It later developed into a designers' and test pilots' convention with more senior officers present, including the vice chief of the Air Staff.

This convention was valuable to us in many ways. The opinions of different firms' test pilots and the RAF operational pilots together with our own, ensured a deeper understanding of the problems being encountered and pointed to the developments we should be pursuing for the future. It gave our designers a broader view and enabled them to understand the practicalities the engines had to contend with. Designers tended to be removed from the total aircraft concept and think of an engine as an engine rather than as a part of a whole weapons system. The meetings were a real way of getting alongside the customer! The cream of the fighter-command pilots used to circulate through CFE and so it was a splendid opportunity of getting to know new people and keeping in touch with one's old friends, and this included some pilots from our allies.

One of the problems that had to be faced early in the fifties was how to continue to attract sufficient government financial support for research and development. As engines and aircraft became more complex their development became more expensive; unless sufficient government funds could be obtained, then advanced technology would suffer. Technical competition with the United States would not be able to be maintained, with consequent loss of the share of the world market for reequipment of the emerging air forces. It was becoming clear that there were too many engine firms and aircraft firms trying for a share of the cake, and it was becoming a rather small cake anyway!

The Ministry of Technology tried to apportion the cake as fairly as they could amongst the many firms, but there were just not enough new requirements to justify so many separate companies. A movement was started to prune down the industry by awarding design contracts to various consortia of companies who would agree to pool their resources; in this way firms began to lose their identities by being merged into larger groups. Hence the British Aircraft Corporation was formed by Vickers-Armstrongs Supermarine, English Electric, Bristol and Percival Aircraft. The Hawker-Siddeley Group was formed by the amalgamation of Hawker Aircraft, Gloster Aircraft, Armstrong-Whitworth, De Havilland and Folland. Handley-Page stood out alone and was eventually squeezed into liquidation.

On the engine side, Bristol and De Havilland engines joined together with Siddeley engines and Blackburn's engine division. Rolls-Royce bought Napier; thus there were two major engine firms and two major aircraft groups, leaving Short and Westlands, who had digested Fairey Aviation, outside the ring. This activity certainly made it easier to select contractors to tender for the available projects.

On the engine side, the competition for funds was as intensive as ever. The Bristol-Siddeley engine group, which had conformed to the ministry's dictum of merger, seemed to be gaining disproportionate funds for new military aero engine projects, while Rolls-Royce, who was more independent and more involved with the expanding civil market and who was embarked on a more ambitious program, was forced to use its own financial resources in order to compete successfully with its friends and rivals in the United States. Eventually, Rolls-Royce bought up the Bristol-Siddeley engine company and so there came to be only one British engine company, the state of affairs today. But the reader should understand how intense this fight for support and for the available military contracts was at the time; it was further accentuated by the fact that Rolls-Royce also needed a share of the American market to maintain full utilization of its resources and manpower.

The reequipment of the European air forces after the war mainly consisted of De Havilland Vampires and Gloster Meteors from Britain. The United States was supplying Republic F-84s, Lockheed Shooting Stars and North American F-100s from surplus stock. The first head-on clash between the main aircraft-producing countries was for the German air force order, which specified a requirement for a Mach 2 supersonic fighter. The contestants for this were from the United States, Great Britain, France and Sweden. Whoever won this competition was likely to obtain the orders also from Belgium and Holland. Many other countries, too, were likely to follow suit, for there was to be a cooperative manufacturing arrangement with the object of gaining manufacturing experience and employment. The British were offering the Lightning, the Saunders-Roe 177; France put forward the Mirage, the Swedes the Draken and America the Lockheed F-104; LTV the Crusader, Grumman the F-11-F and Republic the Thunderchief F-105. The engine companies involved were Rolls-Royce, Bristol and De Havilland from Britain; SNECMA from France; and Pratt and Whitney and General Electric from the United States. It was a real free-for-all.

I had been in the United States to visit Grumman, trying to persuade them to fit the Avon in the Grumman F-11-F; this would have made a splendid aeroplane with an equal performance to the F-104, but much safer. We offered the Rolls Conway to Republic and to LTV for the Crusader 3; we did not offer an engine for the

F-104 on account of its poor safety record and because it had been turned down by the USAF.

Bristol was offering the Olympus to Republic, Pratt and Whitney and GE were already entrenched in United States aircraft. The French would not agree to the Avon being offered in the Mirage for sale in Europe because they preferred the inferior Atar engine because it was French! The Swedes already had the Avon fitted in the Draken. The Saunders-Roe was the favored British submission and used a De Havilland Gyron Junior plus a rocket motor. We were able to displace the Gyron with the Avon in the final submission; and the Germans finally drew up a short list of three aircraft: the American Lockheed F-104, the French Dassault Mirage and the British Saro 177. Ironically, while this critical decision was pending, the British government decided to cancel their order for the Saro 177 on the grounds of economy; they had decided to cut back fighters and replace them with guided missiles. When the minister went to Bonn to talk to his German counterpart and told him that he would not cancel the government order if the Germans would buy it, he was politely told what he could do with it. So that was the end of that promising aeroplane! Because of the lack of performance with the French engine, the Mirage too was turned down, and so the Lockheed F-104 was chosen by the Germans. The Dutch, Belgian, and Italian contracts followed the German, which made it a very large order indeed for Lockheed, especially for an aircraft that had not at that time been bought in its country of origin! By that stroke, Lockheed and General Electric became firmly entrenched in Europe.

This choice by the Germans was later to be seen as unfortunate because the accident rate of the F-104 became very high. I quote from Jack Gee's book *Mirage—War Plane of the World*. He writes:

Accidents are inevitable whenever an air force has to familiarize itself with a new aircraft, but in the 1960s the Luftwaffe, which had ordered over nine hundred F-104 Starfighters, was losing planes and pilots at the rate of one every two weeks; one veteran pilot commented grimly, "Not even the

Spitfire shot down our Messerschmitts so fast." The death roll became the subject of nationwide debate. It is only fair to say that the German version of the aeroplane weighed nine tons due to carrying extra electronic gear, whereas other versions were flying at several thousand pounds lighter weight; also poor maintenance played a part, together with hurried pilot training. The Mirage or the Grumman F-11-F Tiger would have been a better choice.

The battle for the German order had been ruthless. One company issued a brochure giving details of all the accidents that had occurred to one of its competitors, with photos of the pilots and descriptions of the consequences for their wives and families. This was to come to the notice of the German public and was intended to sway public opinion. The representatives of the different firms were billeted at the Konigshof Hotel in Bonn, and it reminded me of Lisbon during the war, a wasp's nest of spies. Most companies were pretty amateur at the selling game, except for Lockheed, who were indeed highly professional. Corky Meyer of Grumman and I tried our best to sell the Grumman F-11-F Tiger with the Avon engine but we were no match for the Lockheed team, who had their top directors and lots of finance available to back their submission; the hotel in Bonn was nicknamed the "Lockheedshoff."

Because Europe had become committed to the F-104 Starfighter, the Commonwealth countries were the next to be courted. I was very keen to get Rolls-Royce engines adopted, particularly since we had captured many world markets in subsonic fighters with the Hawker Hunter using the Avon. It looked as though we would miss out on the first round of supersonic aircraft. We had to find a better aeroplane than the Starfighter to support our engine. We had, unfortunately, fallen behind on the development of afterburners, due partly to the ministry supporting with money the Bristol company and not Rolls-Royce. There now seemed a real chance that we would be frozen out of the fighter market. The Dassault Mirage seemed to be a worthy contender to compete with Lockheed. I went over to Paris and discussed Rolls-Royce engines with Henri Deplante, the chief engineer, pointing out the serious-

The Kestrel-powered Hawker Hart. Many of the RAFs Battle of Britain pilots trained on these biplanes.

The author in his flight suit at the Hendon Air Pageant, 1934.
(*From the author's personal collection*)

The author flying the Rolls-Royce Kestrel-powered Heinkel He 70 in 1936.
(*From the author's personal collection*)

Sectioned view of the twelve-cylinder Merlin.

The Merlin 113 which powered certain De Havilland Mosquito
aircraft. It developed 1,430 horsepower at 27,250 feet.

The Spitfire IX powered with a Merlin 61 of 1,565 horsepower.
It had a speed of four hundred miles per hour at operational
heights, circa 1943.

Whoops! The author's first practice landing on an aircraft carrier. The tail hook of the Sea Hurricane missed the arrester wires and he went through the barrier. (*H.M.S. Ravager official photograph, copyright* Crown)

Britain's most successful bomber in World War II, the Avro Lancaster powered with four Merlins.

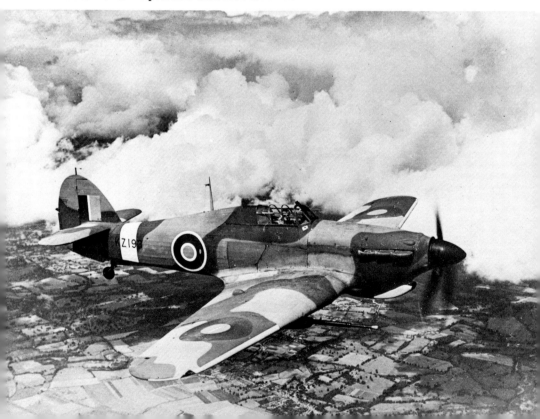

Hawker Hurricane powered with the Merlin 20.

De Havilland Mosquito, the RAFs fastest multi-role aircraft in World War II.
(*Support Graphics Ltd.*)

North American Mustang P-51B powered with a Packard-built Rolls-Royce Merlin.

Mustang IIIs powered with Packard V-1650/3
Merlins.

RAF Westland Wyvern with contra-rotating propellers powered by the
twenty-four-cylinder forty-six-liter (2806 cubic inches), 3,400-horse-
power Rolls-Royce Eagle, last of the piston engines, circa 1944.

The Rolls-Royce Derwent I jet engine (circa 1945) which succeeded
the Rolls-Royce Welland, the first Rolls-Royce jet developed from the
original Whittle WTB design. The Derwent had a double-sided
centrifugal compressor.

RAF Canberra Mk.8 jet bomber powered with two Rolls-Royce Avon
axial flow jet engines. The Canberra first flew in 1954 and many are
still in service (1979).

The Hawker Hunter Mk.6 fighter powered with the Rolls-Royce Avon RA-14
turbojet having a thrust of ten thousand
pounds (4,536 kilograms). The Hunter,
first commissioned by the RAF in 1951,
was sold to thirteen other countries and
many are still in service (1979).

De Havilland Sea Vixen all-weather
fighters, first commissioned by Britain's
Royal Navy in 1959. The Sea Vixen is
powered by two Rolls-Royce Avons.

U.S. Navy Grumman Panther fighters. Early versions were
powered with the Pratt and Whitney J-42, the Rolls-Royce Nene
built under license; later models of the Panther had the J-48,
Pratt and Whitney version of the Rolls-Royce Tay.

The Rolls-Royce Avon-powered Dassault Mirage fighter, intended for
the Royal Australian Air Force.

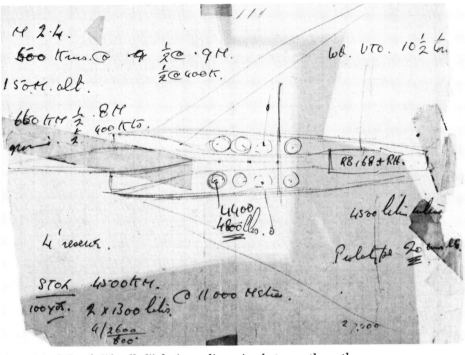

An original sketch "doodled" during a discussion between the author and Henri Deplante of Avions Marcel Dassault which led to the experimental development of the V/STOL Balzac of the French manufacturer, also the Mirage III-V which used eight Rolls-Royce RB-162 (or five RB-145) engines for jet lift. (*From the author's personal collection*)

The Dassault Balzac making a vertical takeoff.

The Hawker Harrier VTOL fighter powered by a single Rolls-Royce
Bristol Pegasus turbojet. Harriers are in operation with the RAF, the
U.S. Marine Corps, and the Spanish air force.

Sectioned view of the Rolls-Royce Spey turbofan engine. The Spey
went into service in 1960 with a thrust of ten thousand pounds (4,536
kilograms); recent models have a thrust of seventeen thousand pounds
(7,711 kilograms). A military version of the Spey is manufactured in the
United States under license by the Allison division of General Motors.

The Rolls-Royce RB-211/524 engine of the Lockheed
L-1011 TriStar. This three-spool turbofan has a thrust
of fifty thousand pounds (22,680 kilograms).

Ernest Walter Hives (1886–
1965). "He made Rolls-Royce
He was director and general
manager during the developm
of the Merlin and the critical
years of World War II, becom
ing executive chairman in 194
Elevated to the peerage in 19
as First Baron of Duffield, Lo
Hives was better known to his
staff as "Hs" or "The Baron."
He retired January 1957, age

Lord Hives examines a compressor disc at Svenska Flygmotor with
G. Gudmundson (left), Flygmotor's technical director, and the author
(right). (Rolls-Royce News, Harker Sales, London)

Sir George Edwards (left), chairman of the British Aircraft Corporation, receives from Lord Boyd-Carpenter, chairman of the British Civil Aviation Authority, the Certificate of Airworthiness for the Concorde. The Anglo-French SST is powered with four Rolls-Royce Bristol Olympus 593 engines. (*Central Press Photos, Ltd., London*)

Willoughby Lappin, who joined Rolls-Royce in 1917, Cyril Lovesey (center), deputy director of engineering, and Sir Stanley Hooker (right), technical director, admire oil painting depicting sinking of the Nazi battleship *Turpitz* at Tromso, Norway, September 1944, by twelve-thousand-pound bombs from RAF Lancasters.

(Left to right) The author, Air Vice Marshal Sir Colin Scragg, Air Marshal Sir Christopher Hartley, Adrian A. Lombard, Rolls-Royce director of engineering, and Cyril Lovesey, deputy director of engineering, on the occasion of a conference in December 1963, to discuss future projects and requirements for the RAF.

Ronald W. Harker with his family in front of Buckingham Palace; (from left) daughter Briony, wife Marjorie, the author, daughter Cherry. (*From the author's personal collection*)

ness of letting Lockheed capture the world market for supersonic fighters. His attitude at first was very disappointing, in that he thought the Atar engine was good enough and as it was French it had to be used anyway! He thought the Avon would be too heavy, that the air intake required would be too big and that the afterburner was too small!

I returned to Derby feeling a trifle depressed. I talked to my old colleague Tom Kerry, who was the chief designer on installations, and asked him to look at the installation of the Avon in the Mirage and see if it was as bad as Henri Deplante had said. Tom had to be careful how much time he put in on this study as his chief, Adrian Lombard, was heavily involved with an attempt to penetrate the American civil market with the Conway bypass engine, which he hoped would be adopted for the Douglas DC-8 and Boeing 707. When he saw Tom with drawings of the Mirage on his board, he rebuked him, telling him not to waste time but to get on with the civil projects.

Tom, however, soon came up with a general arrangement drawing of the Avon Mirage which looked good, and so we asked Challier to estimate the performance. This, too, showed a considerable improvement over the French-engined aircraft, particularly on range. Tom and I then went over to Dassault again; this time Henri was much more amenable and having looked at the drawing was soon saying, "No problem, no problem, the air intake can be made so! The afterburner is not too big; yes we can do it, but who will pay?" Rather like a repetition of the Mustang story, I managed to persuade Sir Denning Pearson, who had been made managing director when Lord Hives became chairman, to come over to Paris to see Monsieur Dassault himself and see if some agreement could be reached whereby a prototype could be built to compete with the Starfighter to our mutual benefit. It was agreed that Dassault would provide the airframe, Rolls-Royce would supply the engine and afterburner and we would go equal shares on the cost of the flight trials.

I was sent off to Australia to talk to the Air Staff about their future requirements for a fighter to replace their Avon-powered Sabres. It was early February 1958 and they hoped to make up their minds by the end of the year; they were studying several types of supersonic fighters, the main consideration being that a range of two thousand nautical miles was necessary to fly from Darwin, over Indonesia, to Singapore, nonstop.

On my return, we looked at the Mirage in this respect and found that if it could be fitted with two 240-gallon ferry tanks it could meet the requirement. The Atar version could not because of its inferior fuel consumption; nor could the Starfighter. I went back to Australia accompanied by Commandant Bernard Waquet, a French naval officer seconded to Dassault as sales manager. One of the conditions of the Pearson/Dassault agreement was that Rolls would not try to interfere with SNECMA selling the Atar engine in Europe and the French would assist Rolls to sell in the Commonwealth countries. Nevertheless, I was not allowed to see the brochure of the Atar Mirage, only the Avon one; this was rather one-sided, I felt!

We arrived just in time to learn that the Australians were going to announce the purchase of the Starfighter within a few weeks. Waquet and I saw all the Australian officials from the prime minister downwards showing them that only the Avon Mirage could fly nonstop to Singapore. They decided to have a rethink and postponed their decision until after a technical mission led by Air Marshal Sir Frederick Sherger, the chief of Air Staff, could visit Lockheed in America and Dassault and Rolls-Royce in Europe. The outcome of this investigation was that they would order the Mirage; we were delighted. It was agreed that a decision on the engine would be made after the completion of the flight trials. The Avon performed well and conformed to its estimated performance. I went back to Australia to be there when the decision was made. Alas, it went against the Avon. It was hard to understand why since the Atar version was inferior.

After research into the reasons, there appeared to be several rather odd factors which determined the result. The French did not realize that there were twenty-five Australian shillings to a British pound; both the French and British were quoting prices in English pounds when suddenly the French realized the difference between Australian and English currency and switched their quote to Australian pounds, giving the appearance of becoming 20 percent cheaper. They could afford to do this as SNECMA was a French-government-owned concern and, therefore, not strictly commercial; they also had a deal going whereby they bought wine and wool as a trade-off for the Mirages.

On the technical side, the Australians had had the experience of buying nonstandard aircraft in the past with the Nene Vampire and the Avon Sabre, both of which had had certain defects; so, they now thought it would be better to buy the same equipment as the French air force; and, lastly, Rolls had offered a larger afterburner that gave an improved performance but would be an added cost. We were told that had Rolls been willing to supply this at no extra cost, they would have chosen the Avon. It was felt that it would be too costly to do this for an order of only thirty aircraft, although some of us were pretty certain the order would be extended far beyond this. Following this, Dassault gained the Swiss and South African orders and eventually very many more. What a great opportunity was lost to us! We consoled ourselves that at any rate the Lockheed F-104 monopoly had been broken and perhaps a number of lives saved! Rolls had not been heartily behind the project as their sights were at this time firmly on the American civil market.

Breaking into the American civil market was the ambition of the Rolls-Royce management. The military side of aviation was becoming rather static; the market was not likely to expand as fast as the civil, and so more attention was being paid to the latter. I believe this was partly because business executives understood the civil market and the people involved; whereas they did not fully understand people in uniform or feel at ease with them. We had been very successful with the Dart engine in the Vickers Viscount; it had sold well abroad and had penetrated the United States market, followed by the Sud Caravelle with the Avon, which had also been bought in the States. The British civil market alone was not nearly big enough to sustain the company, nor were the British aircraft companies who were not very successful in building or selling civil aircraft for export.

The future of the company now depended on·gaining a fair share of the American market, and so a maximum effort was made to achieve this. The Avon had displaced the De Havilland Ghost from the Comet. This version was the first jet airliner to open up a regular service across the Atlantic, beating the Boeing 707 by some weeks. The Conway had been designed specifically for airline operation, being a bypass engine which gave a lower fuel consumption than a straight jet. It was selected by several airlines to be installed in their Douglas DC-8s and Boeing 707s; but the American airlines preferred to stay with Pratt and Whitney. This then became the challenge: could Rolls compete on the American home market against Pratt and Whitney? The battle continues today: it has been long and hard and although a deep penetration has been made by the Rolls-Royce RB211 engine, it broke the company to do it; that, however, is another story.

CHAPTER 17

Vertical Takeoff

I HAD by now become firmly entrenched in the London office as the military aviation adviser to the chief executive of Rolls-Royce. The latter post was now held by James Denning Pearson (Psn) whom Lord Hives had appointed as his successor. Pearson later received a knighthood and became chairman of the company. I remember the dinner Lord Hives gave for thirty-year members of the company, at which he announced his appointment of Pearson as general manager and chief executive. He said that Pearson had been through the furnace and come out shining bright, that he would carry on the leadership of the company and uphold its traditions in a rapidly changing world.

Pearson had started in the design department, had run the Glasgow factory, and gained experience in Canada on the commercial side, thus combining engineering with management. Being a Whitworth Scholar, he could well make full use of these experiences. His was the difficult task to follow the footsteps of the "Maestro" and adjust the company outlook for the postwar entry into civil aviation.

The company had a full order book; its products were spread

worldwide and it was expanding. The military side following the Avon in the Hunter, the Swift, and Canberra, which formed the equipment of many of the world's air forces, was booming. The Avon was the engine in the Vickers Valiant which was the first of the new V-bombers for the RAF; in a supersonic form, the Avon powered the English Electric Lightning.

At this point, I became rather apprehensive about the future, as the Avon was now being closely challenged by the General Electric J-79 engine. This engine had benefited from a great deal of American research and development money and also it had much supersonic experience, whereas the Avon had little. This made it difficult for the Avon to compete for the next generation of fighters.

A great opportunity was missed when the Air Ministry cancelled the thin-wing Hawker Hunter; this had been intended as a replacement for the standard RAF Hunter and was meant to fly supersonically. It would have replaced the many hundred Hunters sold abroad and this would most likely have stopped the wholesale purchase of Lockheed Starfighters and Dassault Mirages, at least for several years. The prototype was nearly complete when the cancellation was announced. We at Rolls-Royce tried hard to persuade Hawker to spend their own money to continue the program, for it would have been an outlet for a reheated supersonic Avon; but in spite of Sir Sidney Camm's vote to continue and Rolls-Royce's willingness to help, the accountants won the day and were content to produce the standard subsonic version as long as it would sell.

Another worry to me, since my job was to promote military aviation, was that civil expansion was receiving greater priority and the future of the military side was being neglected. This, I thought, contributed to losing the Australian engine order for the Mirage. One encouraging factor, however, was the interest that Adrian Lombard, our design director, was taking in the design and promotion of ultralightweight lift engines intended for vertical takeoff and landing (VTOL) projects, now beginning to receive government support.

The VTOL project started when Doctor Griffiths, an eminent research scientist from the Royal Aeronautical Establishment at Farnborough, joined Rolls-Royce to form a forward-thinking department. This was situated away from the factory where Griffiths could dream up advanced projects away from the day-to-day stresses of the work routine. It was he who had designed the first pure Rolls-Royce gas turbine, which I described earlier. Once gas turbines became established and produced a reasonable thrust for a light weight, Griffiths foresaw the possibilities of VTOL by means of mounting engines vertically. He and his team designed a light-weight engine, the RB-108, with a power/weight ratio of 8:1. The proposal was submitted that a battery of these engines could practically replace the wing for lift and the addition of a small number would suffice for forward propulsion.

Griffiths wrote papers expounding his philosophy and gave lectures. These kindled the imagination of the Air Ministry and of the aircraft firms, a number of which were stimulated to do preliminary designs. This was the beginning. One of the problems was the control of such aircraft. In order to test this, a rig was designed and built at Hucknall featuring two Nene engines. This contraption, called the "flying bedstead," was tethered loosely to the ground for its initial flights to prove the stabilization control. Once we knew it worked, it was then flown by Ronnie Shepherd in free-flight. It was followed by a special aircraft built by Short, the SC-1, which used four RB-108 engines mounted vertically and one for propulsion, mounted horizontally for forward flight. This aircraft flown by Tom Brooke-Smith demonstrated satisfactorily that the principle was sound.

NATO issued a specification called NBMR-3 for a supersonic vertical takeoff and landing fighter which attracted submissions from many firms in many NATO countries. There were two main schools of thought on the best way to accomplish the object. The Rolls-Royce method of direct lift was by using a number of vertically mounted lift engines as demonstrated by the Short SC-1; the competing Bristol method was by using a large bypass engine having four variable vectoring thrust nozzles, which could be controlled to give vertical and/or horizontal flight.

Bristol had obtained a financial grant from the MWDP (Mutual Weapons Development Programme); this was actually a grant from the United States government to finance European projects which were considered to be of value for the defense of Europe. It also enabled the United States to buy into European technology since there were strings attached which gave the United States certain rights. The Bristol method was also being supported by the British government as a power plant for the Hawker P-1127 Kestrel which was a subsonic V/STOL aeroplane of interest to the Royal Navy and the Royal Air Force.

Rolls-Royce, on the other hand, had received a contract to design and build the RB-162 engine, a development from the original lightweight lift engine the RB-108, but producing a power/weight ratio of 16:1, a great improvement over the 8:1 ratio of the RB-108. The new engine had many unique features such as a fiberglass compressor casing that considerably reduced the weight. As yet there was no aircraft project to which the engine was allocated.

We were thus at a considerable disadvantage in this forthcoming competition, as we were not being supported by the government. Lombard and I visited Sir Sidney Camm to try and persuade him to consider the RB-162 engines instead of the Bristol Pegasus but he was not interested. Lombard was in dialogue with the French Sud company concerning a rather elegant design based on six RB-162 engines as a submission for the NBMR-3 competition. I was rather enchanted at the time with the Dassault people, as I thought they had political pull as well as great engineering ability, so I went to see Henri Deplante and suggested to him that since he already had a first-class supersonic aircraft in the Mirage, why not fit two RB-153 engines on bomb pilons under the wings; the RB-153 engine was being designed for the Germans as a lightweight supersonic engine.

My idea was to have these engines swivelling so that they would augment the thrust of the propulsive engine and so achieve a total thrust in excess of unity and enable the aircraft to take off in a very short distance; in level flight they would enhance the level-speed performance. This was to be an intermediate step before building a new aircraft to meet the NBMR-3 specification.

A preliminary design was prepared and a meeting arranged to show it to Monsieur Dassault for his approval. This was the beginning of a rather extraordinary chain of events which might have affected the careers of several of us! Present at this meeting were Monsieur Dassault himself, accompanied by his general manager Monsieur Valliers, Henri Deplante, Monsieur Cabriere, the Rolls-Royce representative in Paris, Sam Massey-Cross, and Commandant Waquet and myself.

When the drawing was produced, Marcel Dassault said through the interpreter, "Why do you think I should do this?" I explained my ideas, adding that as the runways in Europe were all targeted by the Russian missiles it was important to be able to rise vertically from roads and other suitable places. He replied, "Why should you redesign my beautiful aeroplane? People will think if I do this it is no longer a good plane. I design my own aeroplanes." With this he got up and walked out of the office. There was a deadly hush and I noticed a frigid atmosphere; but not having understood what had been said in French, I just felt a little disappointed at the apparent unsatisfactory outcome of the meeting.

Then Waquet told me that Dassault was furious, and that he would probably be sent back to the navy for supporting my scheme and that I would not be invited back to Dassault, ever! Before I left for home, I had a talk with Henri Deplante about how to fit some RB-162 engines to the Mirage since Dassault had not liked the intermediate scheme; and from these early sketches the VTO Balzac emerged, to be followed later by the Mirage 3V.

A week after this disastrous meeting, Dassault sent for me and for Lombard and David Huddie, the Rolls-Royce managing director; I decided not to turn up! When Huddie and Lombard returned to Derby they were not at all pleased either, as Dassault had said to them "Where is Harker? I want him to see my new design." I was told to go back to Paris to see him. There he told me, "I have decided to design the aeroplane properly and bury the engines in the fuselage; do you think the RAF will like it?" This then became the Dassault/Rolls-Royce submission for the NBMR-3 and the main competitor to the Hawker/Bristol submission.

All other proposals were now eliminated, leaving only the Mirage 3V which had been flown and achieved vertical takeoff and landing and a speed in excess of Mach 2, together with the Hawker P-1154. But the United States, who was footing the bill, finally decided to cancel the competition because in their opinion the state of the art of V/STOL was not sufficiently advanced to warrant the very large sums of money involved.

The French also, because of the cost, decided not to proceed beyond building two prototypes. The British ministry, on the other hand, wrote out a joint RAF and RN specification for the P-1154 to replace its subsonic fighters. The P-1154 had a configuration similar to the original P-1127 Kestrel, but in order to fly supersonic a much larger engine was to be used, the BS-100, which now became funded by the ministry. This was a serious blow to Rolls-Royce, which was then approached to build parts of the engine under subcontract. This was most unpalatable and reminiscent of Sir Henry Royce being asked to build, during the First World War, engines other than of his own design; and also Rolls-Royce did not believe at that time that one engine with vectored thrust was the best way of achieving vertical takeoff. It also meant that the future British fighter market which traditionally had been engined mostly by Rolls would now go to Bristol.

I was pondering this situation in my office one day and thought, surely we cannot let this situation go by default; why can't we install two Spey engines with reheat in place of the one BS-100! They would give more thrust and provide twin-engine safety. The Spey was a proven civil engine, so it would be available earlier and was likely to be less costly, also. I sketched out how they might be installed and it seemed feasible; so I went to see my old colleague Geoff Wilde and told him what I had in mind; would he do some work on the project? He agreed to look at it.

In the meantime, I went to see Air Commodore Ian Esplin, who was the director of operational requirements at the Air Ministry, and discussed it with him to see if it was at all reasonable from his point of view. He quickly caught on and agreed that twin-engine safety was desirable. He also said the BS-100 was running late on development and increasing in cost. Thus encouraged and with a preliminary design having been drawn up, I contacted Sir Sidney Camm at Hawker and asked him if he would care to talk about it. He agreed to see us, so Cyril Lovesey and Geoff Wilde and I paid him a visit at Kingston. He gave us one of his pep talks for which he was quite famous, saying: Why had Rolls-Royce neglected him for so long?—it was traditional for Hawker and Rolls-Royce to provide aeroplanes for the Royal Air Force; Bristol was good but did not provide the answers in the way that Rolls-Royce did.

This was a good start and then the criticism began. How can you cross over the jet pipes in the required short distance, and so on; anyway it was agreed for both Hawker and Rolls to cooperate on the design.

The Air Ministry was told officially what we were doing and so a big months-long debate started. This new proposal went against the ministry's policy of supporting Bristol and the BS-100 engine; on the other hand the Royal Navy liked the idea of having two engines for safety. Bristol, meantime, was energized to make more rapid progress and finally after much partisan discussion, it was decided to stay with the original proposal. We had certainly rocked the boat, but not upset it, yet.

The general policy of the Ministry of Technology at this time seemed increasingly to be one of supporting Bristol for military projects and Rolls-Royce for the civil ones; this, I suppose was logical, as Rolls had been fairly successful in breaking into the foreign markets with the Dart in the Viscount and Fokker Friendship, and the Avon in the Comet and Caravelle. The Conway was now being installed in the Douglas DC-8 and the Boeing 707, whereas Bristol had only had limited success with the Britannia. Then the Ministry of Technology chose the Bristol

Olympus as the engine for the Concorde rather than the Rolls Conway!

Rolls executives had been paying more attention to the civil projects but were jolted into realization of the possible loss of the military market by being asked to help make the BS-100 engine. It was at the time of trying to launch the double Spey engine for the Hawker P-1154 to supplant the BS-100, that Pearson wrote to the chairman of the Conservative parliamentary aviation committee to emphasize the importance the company now attached to needing financial support for new military projects:

While we have been bending our energies to building up a civil export business, the military business has been going to Bristol-Siddeley, with the result that today we can foresee no new major military project coming to Rolls-Royce, unless, of course, we can substantiate our claims for a twin Spey to replace the BS-100 in the P-1154. Incidentally, the same engine is suitable for the RAF tactical transport which is growing out of the OR-351 requirement. To try to summarize the position, we urgently need a government contribution on a fifty/fifty basis to the development of the R.Co-43 Conway for the super VC-10 to relieve our immediate financial position and in the long term a major military project to redress the balance between our civil and military work, such as the twin Spey in the P-1154 and tactical transport. If we can get neither of these, then the future of Rolls-Royce as an independent firm is grim indeed.

The OR-351 was a tactical transport which could have either the Bristol Pegasus or the Rolls engine, the Pegasus being favored. Both this project and the P-1154 were under consideration by the ministry as to which engine should be selected. After prolonged meditation, we were told that the best solution for both aeroplanes would be with the Rolls engines. This was a great breakthrough for us, but put a strain on the Bristol company. The top men of both companies got together to see if they could agree on an industrial compromise to suit each other. They agreed to suggest to the ministry that Rolls should have the transport engine and let Bristol keep the BS-100 in the fighter.

The navy, meantime, became disenchanted with the progress of the P-1154 and some anticipated shortcomings which were becoming apparent and so they were quietly looking for an alternative aeroplane. The McDonnell F-4 Phantom seemed to be attractive, provided it had the Rolls-Royce Spey fitted. The navy needed the Spey to enable it to meet the naval requirements on takeoff distance from the deck of the aircraft carriers H.M.S. *Eagle* and H.M.S. *Ark Royal* and also to have a respectable combat air patrol time. General Electric did not wish to give in without a struggle and allow the Spey to replace the J-79. They lobbied hard and offered more power but could not meet the requirement—although they tried hard to cut costs and offered a saving in money. It was particularly important to Rolls-Royce to get this order, because it would give an opportunity to develop reheat (afterburners) for the Spey and also to allow Rolls-Royce to stay in the forefront of the military market. It was a narrow run thing, as the following tale will tell.

I was lunching with Admiral Sir Frank Hopkins, who was vice chief of the Naval Staff and responsible for staff requirements; he told me that the defense minister, Dennis Healey, had heard that the Spey was going up in price and was now being quoted at 157 thousand pounds whereas the Rolls quote had been 137 thousand pounds. The ministry technicians had added a twenty-thousand-pound contingency over and above the Rolls fixed price.

This increase put the whole deal in jeopardy, the minister suggesting that navy would have to make do with the General Electric J-79 engine, in spite of it not meeting the full requirement. Sir Denning Pearson and Sir David Huddie were both in Los Angeles talking to Lockheed about the TriStar and the RB-211 engine; so I informed Adrian Lombard of this critical situation. We were able to contact Pearson who decided to return immediately and asked me to arrange a meeting with Dennis Healey. It was scheduled for the following day. Pearson explained that 137 thousand pounds was the carefully considered and fixed price and that the contingency figure added to it was not reasonable. The ministry civil servants would not relent; and so it was necessary in order to reduce the cost that some of the engine specifications be changed. Some very expensive materials in the turbine section were deleted with the result that the top speed was limited. This compromise was eventually agreed upon and the order was placed.

The Royal Air Force was now in the market, as the P-1154 had been cancelled; the requirement was not so critical as that of the navy and they felt that if they bought the cheaper General Electric J-79-engined version they would be able to obtain more aircraft. While this controversy was proceeding, the minister decided to reduce the number of aircraft carriers in the Royal Navy, thus reducing the number of Phantoms they required. The surplus ones were then allocated to the RAF, and that is how it all finished up!

Politicians are the real unknown factor in the procurement of the right equipment for the right job; it happens time and time again that their interference produces detrimental effects on the services. Another example of political shortsightedness concerned the Polaris and the Cruise missiles.

Before the Polaris submarine missile had been decided upon and while it was under development, the United States had decided to produce Skybolt, an air-launched ballistic missile to be carried by the Boeing B-52 bombers of the USAF Strategic Air Command. Britain thought likewise and asked to buy one hundred of them for its V-bomber Force. It seemed sensible to save the cost of duplicating such a weapon.

In 1962, the U.S. Defense Department decided to dispense with Skybolt. It had run into difficulties and had not yet achieved a satisfactory flight; meanwhile, the Polaris had been coming along well. Furthermore, the United States did not intend to have two new deterrent systems, because of the expense. Scrapping Skybolt raised problems: the British would demand adequate compensation; and how would Britain be able to maintain its independent nuclear deterrent? Moreover, the RAF was the instrument of nuclear attack and using the Polaris, if the United States even offered it, would mean the transfer of this responsibility to the Royal Navy. The

Americans did not wish to weaken the Anglo/American Special Relationship Alliance but did desire to loosen Britain's independent nuclear control.

To offer Britain a share in Polaris seemed to be a good political compromise, but instead Britain was offered the opportunity to continue the development of Skybolt alone. Later on, President John F. Kennedy and Prime Minister Harold Macmillan met in Nassau to talk over the issue. Whilst the meeting was in progress, news came through that Skybolt had carried out its first successful air-launched flight! Too late to be of any value in the discussions. The project was scrapped and JFK offered Macmillan Polaris instead. It seemed an extraordinary agreement as the Royal Navy was to have only four Polaris submarines, of which only two could be on patrol at the same time, an easy task for the Soviets to shadow.

The RAF was thus to lose its nuclear deterrent to the Royal Navy. In the interim period, however, until the Polaris submarines could be built, the RAF would have to carry on as best it could. This meant that the V-bombers would have to operate at very low altitude to fly under the enemy radar. They were unsuited to this because of fatigue problems not allowed for in the design; hence their operational lives would be shortened.

The decision was made about Christmas time. I remember I couldn't get the idea out of my head that surely Britain with all her resources and advanced technology could produce a satisfactory solution to the problem on her own. Besides, what was Rolls-Royce going to get out of this? It was known that by flying at low altitude, detection by radar could be avoided; the RAF was already using Blue Steel, a short-range, air-launched missile on the V-bombers. Why not develop a long-range, supersonic low-altitude missile (SLAM) to be carried by the V-bombers. This was after all, only an extension of the German V-1 Doodle bug used during the last war. British industry was certainly capable of developing such a device and it would not be too costly; it would also make us independent of American supplies, which might be unreliable in the event of war.

Also, it would have a Rolls-Royce engine; we had just the very one in the RB-145, a neat little engine that gave two thousand to three-thousand pounds of thrust.

I tried this idea out on my friends at Derby, asking them if it would be possible to go supersonic with a jet engine; other missiles under development had rocket power and therefore had only a short range. The answer from John Keenan, chief designer of the forward-thinking group, was that certainly it is possible if the design of the missile is suitable. He then produced a brochure which showed that one thousand nautical miles was possible flying at Mach 2 with a six hundred-pound nuclear warhead. It would fly at between one hundred and six hundred feet with terrain avoidance and gyro guidance. This I thought was just what the doctor ordered; so to follow the normal routine, I sought the approval of Sir Denning Pearson before peddling it around the industry to find a partner and around the Air Ministry to try and get their agreement to support it as a means of keeping the deterrent in their hands.

I was permitted to do this and after disappointing discussions with the missile-producing firms found encouragement from Professor David Keith Lucas at Short Brothers in Belfast. Marconi-Elliot was keen to produce the necessary guidance system of the required accuracy, and so we endeavored to gain the support at high quarters. I met the air minister with Air Marshal Sir Ronald Lees, deputy chief of the Air Staff; they were both interested, as was the commander in chief of Bomber Command, Air Marshal Sir John Grandy and his senior air staff officer, Paddy Menual; they all saw the point. But then a lunch with Dennis Healey, the Labour shadow cabinet defense minister, was, alas, to no avail. The prime minister had decided the new policy of using Polaris and nothing would change it.

It was a good try. Rolls was always ready to support such enterprising projects, but as Lord Hives once said, "It is no good having bright ideas at the wrong time." We were sixteen years too early! It has now been reinvented by America and called the Cruise missile, but it is only subsonic and, therefore, more vulnerable; it has more accurate guidance but that would have come with time anyway. Just think of the advantages the NATO allies would have had, had it been adopted earlier; the SALT talks with the Soviets would have been different. Now I expect Britain will have to buy such a weapon from America, instead of being able to supply it as a valuable export.

CHAPTER 18

Cancellations

THE Phantom engine contract that Rolls-Royce had received to develop the Spey with its reheat system was a shot in the arm. It provided finance that was badly needed and an incentive to catch up on reheat development, to keep pace with the technology in the United States. But we had to meet stringent deadlines and work within a fixed price budget, a challenge indeed.

The first flight engine was delivered on time and up to specification. It handled well and gave the required thrust. The reheat worked well, also, but the aeroplane was not up to its estimated top speed! This brought up the old chestnut! The aircraft manufacturers, predictably, blamed the engine and we blamed the airframe. The answer was that the base drag of the two large jet pipes had not been properly considered in the performance estimates. This was an aerodynamic problem not well understood at the time. The Lightning suffered from having two jet pipes close together; so did the General Dynamics F-111 and the Mirage IV. The result was that the Spey Phantom was superior on range, on takeoff distance and on climb, but no better on top speed.

Still, installation work proceeded on fitting the Spey into the Phantom. It looked as though Rolls-Royce would get both the OR-351 and the P-1154, and Bristol would be in the back seat. Then fate took a hand in the form of politics. The Conservative government was nearing the end of its term, and its defense policy, as well as the new equipment to go with it, had not yet matured; it was considered by some to be too ambitious and costly. The equipment included the British Aircraft Corporation's TSR-2 (Tactical Strategic Reconaissance), all-purpose supersonic bomber, a vertical (VTOL) or short takeoff and landing (STOL) fighter, the Hawker P-1154, the OR-351, which was a V/STOL transport, and possibly an advanced antisubmarine reconaissance aircraft to replace the Avro Shackleton. All these projects were very advanced and required the latest technology to meet their objectives.

The decision to proceed with these projects happened just before the new Labour government came to power. The first thing Labour did was to cancel them all and construct a defense policy based on the "Island reinforcement" plan, the cornerstone whereby Britain was able to go to the support of all its overseas commitments on short notice. Months later, they decided to withdraw all forces from Singapore and to reduce drastically the size of the Royal Navy by scrapping all the aircraft carriers except the *Ark Royal*.

There was, however, a need to obtain some modern aircraft to replace some of the aging frontline aircraft. So the prime minister, Harold Wilson, backed by Dennis Healey, the new defense minister, went to America to buy aircraft. This seemed an extraordinary thing to do when Britain owned a perfectly good aircraft industry of her own and they needed work! But since the pound had been devalued and badly needed shoring up, the politicans felt that they would go to the States and arrange a bargain whereby the dollar should support the pound and in exchange boost the exports of aircraft from America. At the same time the Americans hoped to eliminate competition from the European aero engine market.

An opinion on this event has been expressed quite forcibly by Stephen Hastings, a member of Parliament, in his book *The Murder of the TSR-2*:

On December sixth and seventh 1965, the prime minister saw President Johnson in Washington at the height of the financial crisis. Backing had to be found for sterling. We know that the vast cost of the American aerospace program was worrying the American administration and MacNamara had resolved to lighten the load by selling American defense equipment abroad. The success of the "hard sell" was already a byword, as witness the export of the Lockheed F-104 Starfighter to Germany and Holland and Belgium and Italy, a moderate but sophisticated aircraft for which the Germans had no easily recognizable requirement in the first place. By now a formidable team of salesmen had been assembled in the Pentagon under Henry J. Kuss, Junior.

The proposition that America's allies should cease to compete with her over military aircraft had been remorselessly plugged in Europe for some years. American resources were so vast that she was bound to win in the end, so why did we British not relax and come to an arrangement by which we should accept a proportion of the total manufacture? I remember hearing it all in Paris from more than one plausible American salesman, both from the industry and the state department as early as 1956. By now the Americans were so keen to break the British aircraft industry that Henry J. Kuss and his colleagues actually offered the C-130 to the British government at a figure several hundred thousands of pounds less than to the Australians for the same aeroplane.

Into this atmosphere of steely determination and supersalesmanship walked a new British prime minister, with little business experience, with a commitment to review all our important aircraft projects, with no manifest concern for British aviation anyway, and with a begging bowl in his hands. It would have been surprising indeed if the Americans had failed to bring off a deal; but, to judge from some reports, even they did not expect the pushover to be quite as simple or extensive as it turned out to be.

This opinion reflects what most of us thought at the time; it will doubtless be some years yet before the Cabinet papers are released for general consumption and the full truth becomes known.

This was the situation the military services and industry found themselves in. We at Rolls were not too concerned about the cancellation of the TSR-2 since it used a Bristol Olympus engine; if our Conway engine had been accepted, as proposed, the aeroplane would have been smaller and had a better fuel consumption. It would have been less costly and therefore might have survived.

But in its place, the Americans offered to sell the General Dynamics F-111 swing wing bomber, in production for the USAF. It had a similar performance and it would be available almost immediately. The Rolls-Royce Spey engine which was being produced for the Phantom was an equivalent engine to the Pratt and Whitney TF-30 engine which the Americans were using. A team from Derby went to Fort Worth to investigate the fitting of the Spey; this was not encouraged by either the United States or the British.

We had another card up our sleeves which was to re-engine the French Dassault Mirage IV with the Spey. Investigation showed this to be completely feasible; the problem was how to overcome British political reluctance to interfere with the British/U.S. plan. I was very closely involved with this and lobbied several members of Parliament on the opposition side to try and upset the government plan. I arranged a meeting with Allen Greenwood and Sir Geoffrey Tuttle of the British Aircraft Corporation to see if they would join Dassault and Rolls-Royce in a consortium to manufacture and promote the Avon Mirage. This would have the advantage of building an aeroplane partly in France and partly in Britain, an aeroplane that would meet the requirement and be as effective as either the TSR-2 or the General Dynamics F-111; it would be much less costly and the currency would be in sterling; it would also provide work for the industry and be available earlier. It seemed to be a good solution.

The RAF gave it serious consideration and sent one of their test pilots over to France to test the Dassault Mirage, which used the less powerful Atar engine; this was just to assess the general performance and handling. The report was favorable. A visit was arranged to Dassault's factory at Toulouse; we took the opposition spokesman on defense with us and had discussions with Monsieur Vallière, the

Dassault general manager. There seemed to be no technical or production difficulty.

We arranged presentations in the House of Commons under the auspices of the Air League; this included one from General Dynamics which the president of the company, my good friend Roger Lewis, led. Questions were asked in the House, such as, "Why is the Spey Mirage IV not being seriously considered rather than the General Dynamics F-111?" No satisfactory answers were given, apart from the minister saying that "the matter was under consideration."

When we did talk to the senior civil servants who were entrusted with the Anglo/U.S. negotiations, they were evasive; even the French air attaché, who was fully in favor of the project, gave us the impression that the matter had been referred to General de Gaulle, the president of France. He considered the odds to be against it. Of course, he must have known at his level that there were overriding considerations of a political nature, of which we were not aware, that made the proposal unacceptable.

Our final attempt, once we had learned that the favorable RAF report had not been allowed to reach the top, was to invoke the Air League once again. The Air League is a nonaligned body of experienced observers of aviation drawn from industry, the services and airlines, who have the best interests of the country and aviation, in particular, at heart. Lombard had just returned from the States with the latest information on the performance and development status of the F-111. It was a dismal story; the aircraft was 25 percent down on performance, running late and suffering from cost overruns.

Air Commodore George Heycock, an old friend who was looking after French interests, and I concocted a telegram to send to the prime minister, whom we knew was having a cabinet meeting to finalize the deal with General Dynamics. I telephoned around to some of the council members of the Air League, of which I was one, to obtain their views, finishing up with the vice chairman, Doctor Bergin, and the chairman, Sir Archibald Hope, an old

Battle of Britain pilot whom I had known in the Auxiliary Air Force. They concurred with this proposal and so we sent the following message to the prime minister:

In view of imminent decision concerning the purchase of F-111 now before cabinet, information relative its shortfall on performance of the order of 25 percent must radically change its acceptability as a cost effective weapon. The Air League submits experienced aviation opinion would view quick decision imprudent in view of new circumstances and no action should be taken until a guarantee of performance, delivery date and cost has been reassessed.

This message was received at the cabinet meeting, we subsequently learned, and the prime minister turned to the defense minister and asked him to verify this and report back within three days. It was confirmed but still the deal went through. A year later, and without an aircraft having been delivered, the British cancelled the deal and lost a considerable amount of money in the process! It really makes a nonsense of buying the right aircraft for the job when it becomes political! The French were badly upset and Anglo/French relations became somewhat strained; this had repercussions very soon on the next project.

The Lockheed C-130 had been chosen in place of the Armstrong-Whitworth AW-681 which had also been cancelled. This really was not a bad decision as the C-130 was an excellent transport aircraft, in satisfactory use not only in the USAF but many air forces round the world. We had previously tried to have the Tyne engine fitted to replace the Allison T-56 and now that Britain was to purchase about sixty-five of them, we tried to repeat the previous exercise. We were not successful primarily because of the cost, although there would have been an improvement in performance. As it has turned out, again it was the right decision to take the standard aircraft as it was.

Now that neither the TSR-2, the F-111, nor the Mirage Spey had been obtained, there was a gap in the strike and reconaissance role. This was filled by the Royal Naval Buccaneer (Rolls-Royce Spey), a subsonic, low-level strike aircraft operated from aircraft carriers; as the carrier force was phased out so they were transferred to the RAF.

The new policy of the Labour government was to foster European cooperation and formulate joint ventures. On the civil side, the Concorde was the prime example; on the military side, there was the Anglo/French AFVG (Advanced Fighter Variable Geometry), the ECAT (European Combat Advanced Trainer) and a variety of helicopters. Much harm had been done to Anglo/French relations by Britain's massive purchase of American equipment and by the rejection of the Spey Mirage IV, in particular. Squabbles between the French and British officials as to which company or country should have design leadership took place with acrimonious statements being pronounced by ministers. General mistrust was rampant and fences had to be mended.

The Rolls-Royce design team and the development engineers, despite all these discouragements, continued to advance technology in the field of turbine engines both for civil and military use. It was appreciated that military planning was illogical and that the way civil aviation was developing was governed by commercial pressures which could be understood; the amount of civil business was expanding and was catching up with the military. This surely was one of the major reasons why it was getting more attention.

The world civil market was poised to place large orders for its aging fleets; the Boeing 707s, Douglas DC-8s, Comets and VC-10s were to be replaced by the much larger Boeing 747 jumbo jets. Boeing had foreseen that with increasing numbers of passengers, larger aeroplanes would be necessary to keep the number of planes down; otherwise congestion in the air and the accident rate would increase alarmingly. Rolls had pioneered a large turbofan engine RB-207 using three shafts instead of two in order to achieve a higher compression ratio. Rolls-Royce hoped to capture a share of the market with this engine, but the time was not yet ripe. It was too big a risk, so the American airlines thought, to abandon Pratt and Whitney, so they used the Pratt and Whitney JT-9D, which was the Rolls-Royce equivalent engine.

A protocol had been signed between Germany, France and Britain to study jointly a European air bus to seat three hundred people and for which the Rolls RB-207 had been proposed (47,500-pound thrust). This was the new three-shaft, advanced technology engine. Pratt and Whitney, the French SNECMA and Bristol had come to an agreement to build the JT-9D engine for sale in Europe. The Americans were studying their own air bus, the Lockheed 1011 and Douglas DC-10. These required a scaled-down engine of 42,000-pound thrust. Rolls preferred to go for the American market and so neglected the European air bus which when built used the General Electric CF6-50 engine. Rolls was selected by Lockheed and Douglas chose the CF6-50, while the Boeing jumbo used the JT-9D.

When Rolls realized that Bristol, their British rival, was flirting with Pratt and Whitney, it hastened their intention to buy Bristol, which they did. This takeover had a big influence on the future. It meant that there was now only one British engine company. This would simplify the government funding of projects and would enable Rolls to pay full attention to penetrating the American civil market. The fact that Rolls and Bristol were merged, their policies made common and people encouraged to work together was not an easy situation because the firms had been rivals for so long and the personnel had grown used to competing against each other. Making the merger work was a challenge to the Rolls directors and Sir Denning Pearson in particular.

This was the atmosphere following the government's flirtation with the United States at the expense of British industry and a policy which the government now tried as an alternative to using British equipment. The slaughter of home activity was nearly complete. The French were not in a forgiving mood and insisted on leadership of any joint project contemplated. The British government was hardly in a position to be firm and so the French had their way, in one case, at least, in a devious way; this was the AFVG, which was to have taken the place of the TSR-2 and the F-111. The French wanted the aircraft to be geared towards air defense, whereas we wished it to be predominantly for strike. The French announced that they would not go along with the project because of cost. It was well known in the industry that Dassault was building, as a private venture, a similar swing wing plane called the Mirage G; this they did and so went on alone.

Now that the AFVG project had come to naught, Britain sought other partners in Europe to build the aircraft. Holland and Belgium declined on the grounds of cost, leaving Germany, Italy and Britain to evolve a joint aircraft. This plan has matured and prototypes are now (1978) under development with promised delivery to the services next year, a gap of thirteen years! The ECAT, christened Jaguar, is now in service both in France and the United Kingdom; it uses two Rolls/Turbomeca engines (the Adour). The helicopters, too, are in use; one of them, the Lynx, uses a specially designed Rolls engine (the Gem). The foregoing is a dismal tale of ineptitude by politicians who should have been better advised by their civil servants; the industry and the Royal Air Force have suffered and wonderful opportunities for export to both France and the United States have been lost.

Having seen the rather confused state of the military situation, the reader must be left with a sense of hopelessness, but strange things do happen. One day an American engineer called at my office on Conduit Street. This was Lyman Josephs, whom I had known and liked when I was working with Chance-Vought trying to persuade them to fit the Conway engine into their Crusader 3 in 1958. We also spent time with each other and our families during a visit to the south of France. He asked me if I could introduce him to the commandant of the School of Air and Land Warfare at Old Sarum; this I was able to do as Air Commodore "Ginger" Weir was also a good friend of mine.

I decided to drive him down in the Bentley for lunch; he wished to discuss a new project that Chance-Vought (now LTV) was putting up for a U.S. Navy competition for a strike aircraft. I knew that they intended to use a Pratt and Whitney TF-30 engine; in fact, that was part of the American specification, so there was little point in trying to suggest using the Spey. However, I did suggest that if ever the design was adopted and went into production, it might have a use in Europe and then perhaps a Spey would have economic and political advantages, as well as having a better performance.

A few years passed and the aircraft named the Corsair was adopted and issued to the United States Navy. The engine had a very sensitive compressor which surged on the slightest provocation, such as ingestion of steam when on the catapult. The result was that on takeoff from the catapult there were several cases of flame out and loss of the aircraft. This caused so much consternation that enquiries were received from the USN as to whether the Spey could be installed. Rolls-Royce and Allison undertook to build the Spey jointly, half in Britain and half in the United States. The Spey gave more thrust and was much less sensitive to air intake effects; the trials were highly satisfactory and a large order for engines was obtained. The USAF also adopted the Corsair. Many hundreds of Anglo/American Speys were built and the aircraft has been highly commended. This was one of those lucky breaks coming at a time when it was badly needed. Sometimes opportunities such as this can be taken at the flood; at other times they appear and the ball is dropped. This happened a few years later, as described in another chapter, and it concerned this same engine, the Allison-Spey.

CHAPTER 19

Anecdotes

THE happenings described in the previous chapter took place between 1955 and 1965, a period of upheaval in the aircraft industry and a time of change in the fighting services. There had been sporadic wars in the Far East and Israel and Egypt in the Middle East. There had been the transition from subsonic fighters to supersonic. Defense policies had drastically changed; civil aviation had expanded and jet airliners had become universal.

All this had had a considerable effect on the Rolls-Royce company. Under Sir Denning Pearson many fundamental changes had taken place, and the work force had greatly increased. Lord Kindersley had been chairman after Lord Hives; then Sir Denning Pearson had succeeded him, carrying on the precedent of having a working engineer as the top man. In spite of all these influences the general theme of the company had changed little underneath, although superficially one might have observed that the executives seemed younger and of a more scientific bent.

Adrian Lombard had instilled an air of pent-up energy in his engineering department and he had a grasp of every detail of his department's many projects. He traveled often to the States where he was highly respected in all aviation circles. Once Lord Hives said to me when he was passing the time of day in my office between appointments: "Lombard is the best engineer in the country and, of course, that means the world." This was quite a statement coming from him; he was not noted for handing out bouquets! I remembered this remark and several years later, when Lombard and I were visiting America together, I mentioned Lord Hives's remark. He was almost speechless with pleasure and asked me to repeat it several times. I felt I had done my good deed for the day!

Serving a long period of time with Rolls-Royce could not but help make one broadminded and averse to doing things like running down one's competitors' products, which some firms, under the guise of good salesmanship, were quite willing to do. If other companies' troubles were brought to the notice of Rolls-Royce top management, the reaction was invariably, "We all have troubles sooner or later, maybe it will be our turn next."

One story which emphasizes this outlook occurred when Stanley Hooker left Rolls and joined the Bristol engine company in 1950. Bristol was in serious trouble with their Proteus turbo-propeller engine. It had several serious defects which were prejudicing the success of the Bristol Britannia transport. Lord Hives and Hooker had not parted on the best of terms, but this did not prevent Hives from telephoning one day saying that he had heard of the troubles and asking if Hooker would like some help. "Just say the word and your old team will be on the next train."

I recall when the competition between Bristol and Rolls was very keen concerning the right philosophy for obtaining vertical lift: was it better to use one large-vectored thrust engine or a number of specially designed light weight engines for lift only. I had met General Parker, who was head of the U.S. Army Air Corps, at the Farnborough Air Show; he had been asking questions about this and I had given him some unbiased answers; I thought nothing about this at the time. A few days afterwards he called to see me at the office and we continued the discussion. I suggested that one method had advantages for some purposes and that the other method was better in other respects. He said he was surprised that I had not tried to condemn the rival product and advocate our own; he then invited me to the United States to give a lecture on vertical takeoff aircraft for the Helicopter Society in St. Louis, of which he was the president. I was highly flattered—and the trip was at the expense of the U.S. Army!

Looking back over the years I was with the company, I can recall with pleasure taking part in a number of interesting projects, some successful and many which were not, as the reader will have noticed. In the course of pursuing these projects, I have traveled widely, visited interesting places, and met delightful people of various nationalities. Many of these visits were to maintain a close relationship with our military customers, particularly with the RAF, and to remind them that no matter how far away they were, Rolls-Royce had their interest at heart.

It was always of value to become acquainted with the environment in which the engines were operating. Conditions differed enormously from cold arctic to sandy tropics, each place affecting our engines differently. Thus, engine problems could be understood in the light of their enviroment and this information conveyed to the engineers back home, who then looked for remedies.

Once when I was staying with Air Marshal Sir Christopher Foxley-Norris, the air officer commanding in Singapore, an amusing incident took place. We had gone to bed fairly early, the A.O.C. being rather tired after a trying day following an action in Borneo where one of his aircraft had been lost. About two o'clock in the morning, Lady Foxley-Norris knocked on my bedroom door and said my wife was on the telephone from England! I spoke to my wife and asked why she had rung up at such an awkward time. She replied that she had been told by her brother-in-law, who had once been in command of a group in Singapore, that it would, due to the time change, be two o'clock in the afternoon! She actually wanted to tell me that only that very afternoon it had been announced in the House of Commons that the Spey Phantom had been ordered. She knew I was due to visit H.M.S. *Eagle* in Singapore harbor the next day and so could tell the admiral the good news. The air marshal, an old friend who, incidentally, wrote the introduction to my last book *Rolls-Royce from the Wings*, took it all in good part and even today it is referred to jokingly.

On another occasion, I was invited to join a proving flight of the first VC-10 on Transport Command to Singapore. Sir Kenneth Cross, who was the commander-in-chief, and I had known each other for many years, dating from 1933 when he was flying Hawker Furies in Twenty-five Squadron and I was flying Hawker Horsleys. We used to meet at the annual training camp at Hawkinge and later when the war started he visited my squadron and I lent him a Hurricane. He was now an air marshal and very kindly asked me to accompany the flight.

All went well until we reached the island of Ghan in the Indian Ocean; I facetiously asked what would happen if we had an engine failure. He said what nonsense; these Rolls Conways could never fail. He shouldn't have said it! For when they tried to start the engines before leaving Ghan, one of them refused to start. It meant the passengers would have to wait for a relief plane from England to enable them to continue the journey. I was permitted to stay on board the VC-10 as a crew member, so we took off on three engines proceeding to Singapore. I was able to send a radio message to the Rolls representative at Singapore asking him to have ready a new fuel-control unit for fitting to the recalcitrant engine. This he did and the aircraft was serviceable the next day before the replacement aircraft arrived from England. Rolls-Royce service was impressive.

Another happy memory comes to mind when I was in Bonn trying to persuade the German Ministry of Defense to buy the Saunders-Roe 177; I heard that Lord Hives was staying at a hotel in Bonn and so I decided to pay him a visit. He had been retired some little while from Rolls-Royce and one of the many honors that he had received was an honorary doctorate of law from Nottingham University. He was there leading a delegation of university professors to Bonn University.

I found him in his room reading a newspaper and having a glass of whiskey. He seemed surprised to see me and asked what I was doing in Bonn; I told him all about the competition between the various firms who were trying to sell equipment to the Germans, which was clearly of interest to him. I asked him if he would care to join me for a meal. He said he would be delighted and could his five professors join us; could I afford it? I said, "Most certainly, I have a rich uncle in Derby who I am sure would be glad to pay the bill!" He was highly amused at that, since he knew we used to call him "Uncle Ernie" and that if his name appeared on the expense sheet there would be no problem! He had a keen sense of humor and with his human touch and puckish wit was always a pleasant companion.

On another occasion, when Hives was still the chairman, he had decided to visit Scandinavia. He asked me to go with him because I knew the various officials in both the services and the aircraft firms. He wished to discuss license agreements for the manufacture of the Avon engine, selected by Sweden for their new generation of fighters. He was very popular with everybody we met, which ensured that we had much generous hospitality and a very enjoyable and busy time.

The Swedish government had recently taken on one of our own test pilots to fly their new prototype Draken which had the Avon engine; he had, unfortunately, been caught by the police driving home after a party and was found to have a little over the limit of alcohol by Swedish law in his blood. It was really very little but Swedish law was very strict and the result was that this pilot had to do a stint in an open-air prison. This is not considered a disgrace in Sweden; in fact, it is a very healthy experience. He shared a hut with a truck driver and a lawyer; they used to chop wood in the forest and lead an outdoor life.

The head of the Swedish Air Force told us that when the new aircraft was readied for its first flight, he had to telephone the governor of the camp and ask him to let the test pilot out for the day to fly the aeroplane, and for subsequent flights. Afterwards in the camp, the pilot would write his report and then wait for the next test flight; the security was tight and what better place than a prison for secrecy? I was also allowed to telephone him in the camp to ask him details about how the engine behaved and whether there were any problems!

CHAPTER 20

The RB-211

THE period 1955 to 1965 had been one of fairly rapid change in the British aero industry. There had been the amalgamation of many aircraft companies into fewer but larger units. There was manipulation by government departments whereby work was shared out according to "Buggins turn next"; there was encroachment into the European markets by the United States and the counterattack to obtain a share of the large civil market in America. This situation was confused by cutbacks in defense spending and vacillation by the airlines, at least the British nationalized ones, in their requirements. But the most serious impediment to steady and logical progress was the political intrigue of various governments.

The effects of the Wilson/Johnson agreement were wearing off, although the feeling between France and Britain on joint aircraft projects was not as cordial as one would have wished. Concorde seemed to be the one area where real collaboration was beginning to take shape but even this project was having a rough ride. In Britain the costs of development were rising and there was an outcry in the press advocating cancellation. Fortunately, the French were more realistic; since it was a joint venture, they put their foot down and would not countenance any interference with the agreed-upon programs.

That is one good thing about multinational projects; once they are agreed upon, and that is difficult enough, they become set in concrete and do not get cancelled. There have been so many instances of purely national projects being scrapped that now, I feel, the only sure way to reach finality is to go for joint ventures. The British popular press is no help at all—except for the aeronautical journals, which do a good job. In my opinion, popular newspapers, or at least some of their aeronautical correspondents, are clearly a menace. Two particular instances come to mind: the Concorde and the Hawker Harrier jump jet. In both cases a correspondent from a Sunday paper week after week brought up all the negative points possible, saying that neither plane would ever go into service, that both were ill conceived and virtually useless. None of the projects' virtues was ever presented. These correspondents are simply biased and ill informed. When both aircraft went into service and the correspondent was wrong, neither the editor nor the correspondent had the grace to accept the situation. This is the sort of thing that does so much harm to aviation.

In the late sixties, the Rolls-Royce motor car division was also making headway. A nuclear division had been set up to work on nuclear reactors for submarines and electric power stations. But in the aero division, there was the challenge to infiltrate the American civil market and the need to maintain a superior position in military aircraft. These two objectives were not going to be easy to achieve under the prevailing circumstances: 1) lack of funding from the government at a time when the cost of more advanced technology was increasing rapidly and 2) lack of such a restriction on our competitors.

This was the situation that prevailed when two very important projects, one civil and one military, became our desired target. If we were successful in landing these projects, it would ensure full order books for the forseeable future, enabling the company to maintain its position of eminence and a high level of employment. If neither project was successfully tendered for, then the outlook was bleak indeed. Rolls-Royce had just bought up the Bristol engine company, which meant competition would come now only from America. The scene was set and the competition was on; the stakes sky-high.

The civil engine project became a competition between Pratt and Whitney and General Electric in America, and Rolls-Royce in Britain. Rolls was working on a large fan engine, the RB-211, designed to meet the wide-bodied transport requirement. Douglas and Lockheed, as aircraft companies, were competing on this plane and all three engine companies were courting their favors. Boeing had already launched the 747 jumbo jet using the Pratt and Whitney JT-9 engine.

While these studies were proceeding in America, another series of long drawn-out discussions had been taking place in Europe between the German, French and British governments for manufacture of the European air bus. This project would require an engine of similar specifications to the one which was required in the States, but rather larger, since it was to be a twin-engined aircraft. Rolls was offering the RB-207, a larger version of the high bypass-ratio fan engine; this was supported by the government as the British contribution to the European venture.

It was clear that both the RB-211 and the RB-207 engines could not be produced at the same time because of the demands of manpower, costs and financial backing; so the Rolls-Royce board decided to concentrate on the American market, since that contract appeared to be more lucrative. On the other hand, the risk was greater because the competition was more severe.

The American airlines seemed to be equally divided in their opinions as to which aircraft and engine to choose: the General Electric CF-6 or the Rolls RB-211 (the Pratt and Whitney JT-9, having been chosen by Boeing, faded out of the wide-bodied three engine aircraft competition). Finally McDonnell-Douglas chose the CF-6 in their DC-10 and Lockheed went for the RB-211 in their TriStar. The market was therefore split and the selling phase to the airlines started. Both aeroplanes attracted orders from the airlines; the DC-10 was getting the lion's share but the TriStar was struggling to catch up. This intensive sales campaign boiled over into Europe, where again the DC-10 gained the advantage. The CF-6 engine was to be built jointly by GE and the French company SNECMA.

In order to obtain these contracts with such severe competition, the companies cut costs to the bone. With hindsight it seems a pity that the two engine companies could not have come to an amicable agreement and engineered a joint venture; there hardly seems room in the world for three engines of similar design and of such prodigious cost. But Rolls-Royce's success in getting this order and penetrating the American civil market with a new engine in a new aeroplane was hailed by everybody—the government, the press and the industry—as a great triumph. David Huddie, the managing director of the aero division, was given a knighthood; he had lived in America for months and conducted negotiations with the airlines and the aircraft companies personally.

Once we had obtained the order, the engine had to be manufactured and produced on a tight schedule, to meet the airlines' demands and the Lockheed program. This contract came soon after the merger with Bristol, but full advantage could not be taken of the potential manpower that this merger implied. Bristol had their own troubles with engine programs they were already engaged in; these were mainly the Olympus engine for the Concorde supersonic airliner and the Pegasus for the RAF's jump jet fighter. While the two companies had been keen rivals for years, now the two divisions had to be brought together and made to work as a team. This was no easy task as personalities were involved. There had been disagreements on engine philosophy which now had to be reconciled and work programs had to be integrated as far as possible; all this was to take time.

The works at Derby was getting organized to put this large RB-211 engine into production. This was a mammoth task; the engine itself was much bigger in overall dimension than anything the company had produced before; it was a different shape and the diameter of the fan was eighty-six inches, which necessitated large machinery to cut the metal and required new techniques in welding. There was also a new material to be developed; this was the new carbon fiber, Hyfil, which had been pioneered by the Royal Aircraft Establishment with collaboration from Rolls-Royce; it was much lighter than aluminum and stronger than steel.

Lockheed officials visited the Derby factory frequently, keeping a close watch on progress; nothing like this had ever happened before. Lockheed was in a precarious financial position; they were fully aware that their future depended on Rolls's delivering the goods on time and up to specification. Rolls's ability to compete successfully on delivery dates with the usual American manufacturers had been one point of considerable doubt with Lockheed, and it had taken a lot of persuasion to overcome their doubts. It was said that Rolls-Royce had too much work on hand and that their resources were strained. It was true that there were a large number of various types of engines in service and also many commitments to be met. This heavy work load was suggested by some critics to be an adverse factor in the selection of the engine and a possible cause of late delivery. Hence Lockheed's insistence on monitoring progress.

I, in my job as military aviation advisor, was always much more interested in the company's performance in the military field. Since my liaison had been so close to the air forces of the world, I began to come under fire from customers who were beginning to notice that they were being neglected. Frequently the military customers now complained: "Why don't you look after us like you do the civil people?" This was fair criticism as spare parts were in short supply, engines were late in being returned to the air force after repair, and aircraft were grounded due to a shortage of spare engines. When various RAF visitors came to the works, they noticed that there were placards up all over the place noting how many days to the delivery of the first engine for Lockheed, while the RAF was in trouble with their programs slipping, which in some cases prejudiced active operations. I decided something should be done to improve matters and even out the Rolls-Royce effort, which should have been equally serving both civil and military customers.

I started a committee, with the blessing of the chief executive, which I called the "Military Aviation Year Committee"; we met frequently and thought up ways in which the situation could be improved. We found that the spares backlog was worst on engines produced by the Bristol division. They had a mixed bag of engines to look after, engines which had been inherited from past mergers. There was the Sapphire, which had been an Armstrong-Siddeley engine, the Blackburn Nimbus, Bristol's own Viper and Olympus, the Pegasus and a number of small helicopter engines, which came from De Havilland and were licensed from General Electric in America. Rolls-Royce was not so badly off since they had only their own engines, although the Tyne turbo-propeller engine was always rather a headache. Also the Royal Air Force and the Ministry of Aviation had been trying to deal with two managing directors— Conway at Bristol and Huddie at Derby—instead of one central source. The confusion was due mostly to the recent merger, of course, and we would have to live with it for some time; in the meanwhile, however, our efficiency had been impaired. This all did not affect the RB-211 position, but it did go against us in the equally difficult task of competing for the next European fighter aircraft engine.

Concerning this very important fighter requirement, the reader will recall that after the cancellation of the TSR-2 and the abortive purchase of the General Dynamics F-111, there had been a lack of interest in an Anglo/French version of the Mirage IV and abandonment of the Anglo/French AFVG (Advanced Fighter Variable Geometry). Time had gone by, and now it was urgent that a new project be started. A consortium was formed among Britain, Germany and Italy to build a swing wing strike fighter, called the MRCA (Multi Role Combat Aircraft), now known as the Tornado. The object of this aircraft was to supercede existing fighters and bombers such as the Phantom, Buccaneer and Vulcan; one aircraft would be able to do the jobs of many.

Because the MRCA was a collaborative effort, it was agreed that the manufacture would be shared among the three countries in proportion to the number of aircraft ordered. The Americans, of course, did not want to relinquish the grip they had won on the European market when they had sold the General Electric J-79 engine and the Lockheed F-104 ten years before. So the same trio was in competition once more: Rolls-Royce, Pratt and Whitney and General Electric.

Geoff Wilde, who was the chief engineer at Derby for future projects, had designed an advanced three-shaft, bypass engine for a strike fighter. Bristol, too, had been developing a competitive engine before the takeover. Now that both companies had come together, a decision had to be made as to which design should be selected. One can imagine the feelings of the two design teams now within the same firm, who had to agree on the better design and make it superior to either of the American designs. All this was happening while the Derby division was struggling to meet the tight production schedule for the RB-211!

A very tragic blow hit the company during this period; Adrian Lombard, our brilliant and popular director of engineering, died suddenly and very unexpectedly of a stroke. He was quite irreplaceable at this time; I am sure that many of the troubles that were to beset the development of the RB-211 could have been overcome sooner had we not lost him.

Sir Denning Pearson set up joint committees on cost engineering and production to make the most of all the talent that was now available. It was decided that the Bristol division should examine Geoff Wilde's RB-199 three-shaft engine and Derby should pass its opinion on Gordon Lewis's two-shaft engine. After much discussion, it was mutually agreed that the three-shaft engine would be the most suitable for the MRCA strike fighter. Pearson accepted this and decided that it should be developed by the Bristol division; this seemed to be a judgment of Solomon.

Then the engine plan was submitted to the three governments concerned and to the design team of PANAVIA, which was the name given to the joint aircraft company. General Electric and Pratt and Whitney also submitted designs, and so the battle was on. GE's design was a straight jet which, although very suitable for a pure fighter, did not give the required range for a low-level strike aircraft. GE was developing their engine for an American fighter specification; so they dropped out, leaving Pratt and Whitney, who was offering a bypass engine similar to the RB-199, but with only two-shafts.

I had become closely involved with this project in my capacity as military aviation advisor, and I was told to treat both divisions of the company equally. This at first I found difficult, as I had for so long been working for Rolls-Royce in competition with Bristol. It took a little time to become impartial, but at least my initial feelings gave me the ability to understand the feelings of the Bristol people, too. I was charged with seeing that the two divisions should work together in harmony! At the time, there was no senior director in charge of this campaign; therefore, the determined effort which David Huddie had put in when going after the RB-211 order was lacking.

I had a close association with the British ministries who were responsible for the international negotiations. Sir William Cook was the chief negotiator backed up by Mr. Handel Davies, an old friend of mine of many years standing, and Air Marshal Sir Mike Giddings. We were in constant touch and so I knew exactly how things were progressing in Germany and what our chances were. The news was not good: the Pratt and Whitney engine was gaining in favor, due not to technical superiority but to damaging propaganda. Interested parties whispered that Rolls-Royce was overcommitted on other projects and the RB-211 in particular; also the resources of the American manufacturers were said to be superior and this was an important factor in developing such a sophisticated engine.

These items of propaganda were passed on to me and I reported them to the company. The attention of the senior staff was still focused on the RB-211 and Lockheed TriStar, so that the seriousness of the situation was not appreciated. The Spey Phantom was at this time completing its development in the States and there were certain problems with the reheat system; this intelligence was duly fed into Germany with the suggestion that if Rolls-Royce could not get the reheat working on the Phantom, what chance would they have with the more complicated system on the MRCA?

Acceptance of the Pratt and Whitney engine would have presented certain problems: Because the United States was not in the consortium and would, therefore, not be ordering any aeroplanes, why should they get any work out of it? This could, however, be got over perhaps if the engine were to be built in Germany or Italy or even by Rolls-Royce under license. When I heard this suggestion, the red flag went up and I told Sir Denning that if we did not take the project more seriously, we would be sure to lose.

I arranged a dinner party in London for Sir Denning to meet with Air Chief Marshal Sir John Grandy, the chief of the British Air Staff, and a number of his senior officers who were concerned with operational requirements, and some senior RAF officials. This meeting was ostensibly to explain the Spey Phantom difficulties. But beforehand, I had a talk with Sir John (we had known each other since we were flying officers) who told me that he was very worried about the engine negotiations. It seemed that the consortium might have to agree to accept the Pratt and Whitney engine unless Rolls-Royce really turned on a maximum effort to convince the committee making the choice that all the rumors were unfounded, and that the delivery dates and performance and cost requirements could be fully met. This was really the moment of truth. I asked Sir John to repeat all this during the dinner, so that Sir Denning could hear it from the "horse's mouth"! This he did, in no uncertain words and backed up by his staff. After dinner when the guests had left, I said to Sir Denning that surely we must put someone in charge of the MRCA who will put as much effort into this project as Huddie put into the RB-211.

Sir Denning straightaway telephoned Hugh Conway (the managing director of the Bristol division, which was to develop the engine) at home and put him in sole charge of the enterprise, explaining how serious the situation was and stressing that no time was to be lost. The MRCA committee was then invited to visit each division of the company to see the extensive facilities available; presentations were given, backed up by further visits to the National Gas Turbine Establishment. The committee went away convinced that Rolls was quite capable of meeting all its commitments, both civil and military. Finally, after further meetings and deliberations, the decision was made and the RB-199 was chosen!

I was still trying to get more attention to the RAF's complaints on shortages of spare parts and long delays on overhauls. I thought the best way to do this was to arrange some more confrontations between senior management and the commanders-in-chief of the various commands. A series of visits were arranged, at which both Conway for Bristol and Huddie for Derby, heading a team of service engineers, overhaul and flying staff, could confront at his headquarters each commander-in-chief and his engineering staff. The idea was to have a frank discussion on mutual problems with the result that there would be better understanding of each other's problems and the RAF would get better service.

I was glad to see that the RAF did not pull their punches during these meetings. The Rolls team took due note and promised to do better; but alas, no rapid improvement was forthcoming. It is not possible with a large organization to wave a wand and obtain immediate results. However, the message did get through that the RAF was of equal importance commercially with the civil customer; afterall, the RAF paid over forty million pounds annually to Rolls-Royce for spare parts.

Rolls-Royce management intended, no doubt, to do better with the military; but once back at the factories, they succumbed to the pressure from civil customers and fulfilled the inbred desire to satisfy them first. So there was little or no improvement in servicing the military customer. Promises were made to the ministry to increase the number of overhauls per month in order to catch up on the schedule, but the schedules were not met. Our reputation was suffering.

I arranged another dinner party in London, hoping that it would have the same satisfactory result as that which had worked so well with the RB-199 engine. I thought that if Sir Denning, our chairman, could hear from the heads of the RAF just what they thought, with the two managing directors and production director also present, then what I considered a very serious situation could be remedied.

The dinner party was a pleasant social occasion; but we had been to the Farnborough Air Show and were perhaps a little tired. The party remained on a social level and the Air Board did not, as they did on the previous occasion, voice their true opinions. When they had departed, Sir Denning read the riot act to the Rolls-Royce officials and said there must be a greater effort to meet their obligations and satisfy the RAF since Rolls-Royce and the RAF traditionally had had close, satisfactory and harmonious relations.

Unfortunately, this attention to military problems came too late; the company was getting into a critical situation with cash flow, due to the delays in the development of the RB-211 for Lockheed. There had been a large increase in development cost due to the Hyfil carbon fiber showing up defects which were not anticipated during the "bird ingestion tests." This test involves projecting a four-pound bird at four hundred miles per hour into the intake of the engine, a test which must be successfully withstood by the fan and compressor blades. Unfortunately, the Hyfil blades shattered on impact with the bird. This meant redesigning the fan and changing the material to titanium, thus delaying the whole program and increasing the costs. This very serious situation swamped all other considerations and it was now becoming a question of survival for the company.

I was disappointed at the management's choice of priorities, not knowing the grave situation that was developing. I continued to try to get the middle management of the various divisions to give their best attention to the military overhaul situation. They really tried to do this and I believe the RAF understood that an improvement was not going to be easy; they did appreciate that there was an effort being made, but nobody knew how close we all were to disaster.

Although the MRCA European fighter with the Rolls RB-199 was well underway, there was still a gap in the market for a fighter for those countries which hadn't joined the consortium. These were the smaller countries, who felt that they could not afford such a sophisticated or expensive aeroplane. Australia had also just issued a staff target for an aeroplane to replace their Mirages. I had for some time been an advocate of using booster engines for improving the performance of good existing airframes; the reader will remember my effort to do this with the Mirage, and Monsieur Dassault's reaction! I felt that the time was ripe to try using booster engines again, but for a different reason. A large number of countries were still operating Starfighters and Mirages, both supersonic but now lacking somewhat in what was called SEP (specific energy performance). Briefly, SEP means a higher power-weight ratio, so that the climb performance and maneuverability in tight turns are improved. A good way to get more SEP, aside from designing a new expensive aircraft and engine, was to add a booster engine at the rear of the fuselage, rather like a mini-TriStar. We had just such an engine in the Bristol Viper. If the Viper could be fitted neatly and was aerodynamically feasible, it would provide the necessary SEP for the Starfighters and Mirages and also provide a shorter takeoff. It would be a get-you-home engine in the event of main engine failure.

The Bristol project design office kindly did a brief study which showed that the Viper's performance was attractive and the cost very reasonable; this could mean a great saving in defense funds. It would prolong the life of the existing aircrafts until the next generation. I then visited the Dutch Fokker company, whom I thought might be willing to convert their Starfighters, and also visited the Government Aircraft Factories in Australia, who might wish to do likewise with the Mirages. In neither case did the companies respond; this was due partially to the parent companies' not wishing to investigate this option thoroughly, since it would obviously interfere with their own new expensive projects. It would have been wonderful business for Rolls, though, who would have had large orders for the Viper engine! (It is interesting to note that at this writing, eight years later, the Australians are still in the market for a new fighter.)

On my way back from Australia, I visited several firms in the States. I wanted to try out the booster engine idea on my friends at LTV; they proved to be very interested in developing the Corsair with more SEP. We had a positive discussion which might have led to something; it concerned a developed Spey with a possible reheat system. A developed Spey with afterburner had a great potential; it was an engine that could be used to fall back on if anything prevented the MRCA from coming to fruition. The Spey engine was already in production in collaboration with Allison as a joint venture; it was more advanced than the British version used in the Phantom.

Some of us felt that if the Spey had the British afterburner fitted, it would give about twenty-six thousand pounds of thrust. This would be in the same ball park as the new advanced-technology American engines, designed for the new supersonic fighters which were on the drawing board. We knew that the new Pratt and Whitney engines, the F-100 and F-401, scheduled for the F-14 by Grumman and the F-15 by McDonnell-Douglas, would be lighter—but they were entirely new and would be very costly and very probably late on delivery. The Spey would be much less costly and it could be available at the right time, most likely with only minor development problems because it had already had a lot of service experience. John Hodson, the project engineer at LTV and I visited the Pentagon and talked to General Glasser, suggesting that the United States should fund the Spey engine as an insurance policy in case of delays or cost overruns on the new Pratt and Whitney engines. Glasser was quite willing to consider this if he was given all the necessary information to back up our case. So far so good! We knew that the engine would fit both the F-14 and the F-15, so there would be no difficulty there if the engine became available.

The ground had been prepared; all we needed was agreement from Rolls-Royce management and the British Ministry of Technology to send over the relevant data for study in depth. But the timing was unfortunate; Sir Denning Pearson, the chairman of Rolls-Royce, had stepped down as the company was approaching its financial crisis, and another man assumed, temporarily, the role of chief executive of the aero division. He attended a meeting of my "Future Fighter Committee" where we were recommending action to pursue the Allison Spey. He took the opposite view and forbade any further work on this engine. He said it would clash with the new engine for the European MRCA project. This was quite clearly nonsense, as the RB-199 engine for Europe was being engineered at Bristol and the Spey would be done at Derby and in America.

This decision proved to be a grave error. Subsequent events have shown that had the Spey been developed with the afterburner to give twenty-six thousand pounds thrust, it would have been ready to be installed in both the F-14 and F-15. The new advanced-technology engines by Pratt and Whitney were both late and greatly in excess of their estimated cost. In fact, the F-14 is still using the TF-30 engine, which was scheduled for the first few aircraft only until the F-401 was ready. There is now no British engine of this power and if one is required for any new European project, an American engine will have to be obtained.

CHAPTER 21

The Bankruptcy and Reorganization

WHEN I arrived home from Australia at the end of November, things were changing noticeably at Rolls-Royce. There was an atmosphere of impending doom. I had been away only three weeks; but suddenly people were going about the factory with long faces. Everyone was discussing the RB-211—why it was behind schedule.

The facts were that the RB-211 engine had been offered at a fixed price. Six hundred engines were contracted, but the price did not make sufficient allowance for the unexpected inflation that ensued in the economy or the unanticipated development costs that arose. These were partly due to the need for replacing the Hyfil blades with titanium, which necessitated considerable redesign; but the rapid rate of escalation of labor and material costs, as well as suddenly vastly increased interest rates took everyone by surprise. This all resulted in the usual escalation allowance being grossly inadequate, and consequently, severe losses were expected on the total contract with Lockheed.

How was enough money to be found to pay for the extra development costs? Notes came round from the administration saying that company newspapers were to be cancelled, tea was to be taken in paper cups, all expenses had to be curtailed and—worst of all—the directors' Bentleys were to be sold. My Rolls Bentley Continental, which I had recently had repainted, and which I had arranged to buy at an agreed price upon my retirement, was to be taken over by Conway; he had just been promoted to chief executive of all aero divisions. He was rather partial to vintage cars of character and he owned three Bugattis! He proved to be too long in the leg for the Bentley, so it was put on the market and sold; Conway got a Rover instead. (I finally received some compensation through the courts!) I was offered a Rover, but it never materialized; things were moving very fast now, getting close to the cataract.

The ministry, who had promised forty-seven million pounds to keep the cash flowing and continue the RB-211 development, was now making conditions; they put in an independent firm of accountants to check the Rolls figures. This firm came up with some pessimistic answers which gave the government the excuse to revoke its earlier promises to support the company with the necessary cash. Sir Denning had stepped down from the chair to be replaced by a government nominee, Lord Cole; and several other new members of the board were appointed.

When Lord Cole sent for me to ask me what I did in the firm, I told him that I was the military aviation advisor, that I had been with the company for over forty years, and that my main interest was to look after the interests of the Royal Air Force. He asked me if the RAF were content with the attention they were being given, so I told him quite clearly that they were not! He asked me what I was going to do about it, saying that where he had just come from (Unilever) the customer was always right. I replied that such policy used to be the case at Rolls-Royce, but answering his question, I said that I thought he should make the company's policy to treat the RAF as well as the civil customer was being treated, and that high priority should be given to getting the overhaul situation back on schedule. He thanked me for my suggestions, saying he was having a board meeting that same afternoon.

I felt that a new broom might sweep clean and that the board might be able to accept the advice they were being given. But things had gone too far by this time; within a week, there would be no more money to pay the wages. I and several colleagues suddenly found that we had been let go, and two days later, the company was declared bankrupt.

The receiver was appointed and the government took over all parts of the company—the aero and gas turbine divisions—engaged in defense work. The motor car division was offered to the public and the shares were all duly taken up. A new company was formed named Rolls-Royce Motors Ltd.; the board was reconstituted and the chairman, a well-known banker, Ian Fraser, took over, supported by David Plastow. This company has gone from strength to strength producing new models, many of which go for export; the company is making good profits and maintaining the reputation of the name in all respects.

The bankruptcy itself was a shattering blow to the prestige of Great Britain; it was a national disaster. There was no other company that could have had a more profound effect on the reputation of Britain. Just before the crash, the shares had fallen to around seven pence, but eventually the receiver will have paid the remaining shareholders around fifty-eight pence a share. This makes one feel that perhaps the company should never have been allowed to go bankrupt. I agree that there was a need for streamlining in the works; there were too many people being employed, the overhead was too high and management needed reorganizing. Yet this could have been done without the government taking such drastic steps.

The now nationalized aero engine company went through a very difficult phase immediately after the bankruptcy. Lord Beeching, who had joined the Rolls-Royce board, did tell the prime minister that he believed the RB-211 would be successful and that with an injection of money the company could carry on. Two other board members disagreed; they said that the RB-211 would lose money on the Lockheed order and advised that it should be discontinued. In fact, they were completely wrong. Now, eight years later, the engines sold on the Lockheed order have made a substantial profit and further orders have been placed; other markets have been developed and the American market has been penetrated by re-engining the Boeing 747 with the RB-211 jet for certain customers.

The period immediately after the crash was an unhappy one; morale was low at all levels. Many of the senior officials such as myself, who knew everybody in the industry and who were known worldwide, were made redundant. There was almost nobody left of the old school on the main board of the nationalized aero engine company; apart from Stanley Hooker, they were all new. Fortunately, the engineering quality was still there; the old wartime Merlin team of Lovesey, Hooker, Rubbra and Fred Morley was called in to put the RB-211 to rights; they were all officially retired, but they answered the call and were totally successful.

Reverberations from the bankruptcy and its aftermath went round the world. How could it ever happen? How could it be allowed to happen? Why had all the experienced officials been allowed or forced to leave? Confidence in the new nationalized company, first known as Rolls-Royce (1971) Ltd., fell. None, or at least few, of the senior officials from the airlines, the aviation industry and the RAF knew who they should talk to. Sir Denning had left, Tim Kendall, Stephen Bragg, Sir David Huddie and many others had gone. New people who undertook their tasks were quite unknown, so a gap in customer relations occurred and one wondered how, or if ever, the cherished traditions of the old company could be restored. Accountants, civil servants and administrators had taken over where skilled engineers had predominated before. Fortunately, the middle management, mostly engineers who still had the spirit of the company instilled in them, carried on and produced good engines, keeping up to date with design. But these people were not happy, as of course they felt insecure for the first time in their careers.

The old family bonds and close-knit relationships that had been traditional with Rolls-Royce disappeared overnight with the aero engine company's nationalization. The void was filled not by indigenous personnel well versed in the ways of the great company, but by nominees of the politicians who had decided to nationalize the company. These were good men, obviously having risen to positions of eminence in their various spheres of experience, but Rolls-Royce was just not an ordinary company; traditionally it had been controlled by men of great stature and predominantly by engineers. How can an accountant or an administrator or even a good manager replace an eminent engineer in a company that had risen to the top by engineering excellence and understanding? Sir Denning was the last to combine Rolls-Royce tradition with the ability of a qualified engineer; his training and experience had been handed down from Lord Hives.

The new board consisted of accountants, civil servants, retired RAF officers and businessmen—all remote from the grass roots at the factories—but they endeavored to get things going again. With government finance and backing, the "tumbrill" rolled along the bumpy road. The engineers called out of retirement—Hooker, Lovesey, Rubbra, Morley—saved the day by getting the RB-211 engine through its tests and looking after it in service with the airlines. Lockheed too was in a perilous state at this time—they had been having a very difficult time trying to obtain financial backing in the States to keep solvent. But soon the RB-211 gained the reputation of being the best of the three big fan engines; the engineering reputation of the company was saved.

The problem now was to get the housekeeping right and try to make a profit. The administration of the various divisions was changed several times, which did not add to confidence amongst the staff. I remember visiting the company's chalet at the Paris Air Show in 1973 to see my old colleagues. I was dismayed to find a very low morale amongst them, as they said they did not know from day to day how long they were going to be there and the three aero divisions were still not united.

Upheavals continued for some while until Sir Kenneth Keith, an eminent banker with an international reputation, was made chairman. He understood the intricacies of high finance and how the survival of an indispensable armaments complex had to be related to national politics. He also understood how such a company had to be organized to compete with its American rivals, who had all the advantages of a larger market and ample funds from its government for research and development. He personally selected his team, including some recently retired senior RAF officers of high regard, to assist him in directing the policy of the company, together with Dennis Head, who is the managing director of all aero divisions. The overall control has now become stabilized and the traditional spirit is once more emerging.

In the eight years since the reorganization, there have been many technical successes for the aero company. The RB-199 engine for the MRCA (Tornado) is now in full production, having been selected against severe competition from Pratt and Whitney and General Electric. The Adour engine, installed in the British Aircraft Corporation's Jaguar, is selling well; the Pegasus in the Hawker Harrier has sold in America and is being partly manufactured by Pratt and Whitney. The Gem small helicopter engine has passed all its tests and is in production. New advanced concepts will be developed when funds can be made available. The general picture is one of maintaining a competitive posture worldwide, as recently shown by China taking a license for the Spey for their new fighter.

The Concorde, after much opposition from the American public, has become a symbol of European excellency in aeronautical engineering and continues to operate with reliability and consistency, even if it is not yet a commercial proposition. Rolls-Royce gas turbines have been adapted for Royal Navy frigates and destroyers. There are many industrial applications also.

It has become very clear that the cost of modern aircraft, engines and electronic equipment is so prohibitively high that it was inevitable that single companies can no longer bear the expense; even countries cannot, so what hope did Rolls-Royce have of going it alone? The future is hazy for all companies engaged in producing arms for the military and supplying equipment for the airlines, because these activities are subject to so many imponderable influences.

But with her newly found confidence and with suitable and adequate backing from the British Aerospace Corporation and the government, Rolls-Royce Ltd. will steer a successful course to renewed success. Over the next few years the direction of company policy must change as key people retire; but now the trauma is over and stability has been established once more.

CHAPTER 22

Epilogue

AFTER the receiver was appointed in 1971 to conduct the affairs of Rolls-Royce Ltd. in liquidation, the motor car and oil engine divisions had to be disposed of as shareholder's assets. Mr. Rupert Nicholson, the receiver and liquidator, was also manager of the Rolls-Royce factories, so the existing boards continued to function on his behalf, continuing to carry on production and trade.

The motor car company was making a profit and had been doing so continuously for many years, but the profit had been small when considered against the turnover of the whole company. Mr. Nicholson wisely supported the motor car company directors in planning their future policies; he ensured that all the subcontractors and accessory-makers would be paid and would continue to be paid for delivering their supplies. He also endorsed the launching of the new Corniche car, which was demonstrated to the press in the south of France a few weeks later. This presentation was well received and this new model was thus off to a good start; many hundreds of them have been delivered and they continue to be sold in increasing numbers.

The general situation of Rolls-Royce motor cars continued to improve but there was concern that some finance house or motor car company might make a successful bid for the business and "who knows what might follow and what damage might be done to the name and reputation of the company and its unique products?" By 1973, two years after the crash, profits had increased and Mr. Nicholson was able to offer the shares to the public. The offer was taken up and so the new company, Rolls-Royce Motor Holdings Ltd., became once more the property of public shareholders and was again quoted on the London Stock Exchange as a wholly owned limited company.

Mr. Ian Fraser was elected chairman of the new company, having been chairman of the motor car company under the receiver, since 1971. David Plastow became the managing director, having been directing operations since the liquidation; much credit must go to him as leader of a team that has been going from strength to strength under very difficult circumstances, brought about by general industrial unrest in the British automobile industry. In spite of these problems, the development of new models has been proceeding with great success. With expansion, increased profitability, and the maintenance of the quality of the cars, Rolls-Royce Motors now exports sixty-five percent of its output; so the reputation of Rolls-Royce is enhanced throughout the world.

The turnover in 1971 was £38,354,000, with a profit of £3,825,000. These figures increased steadily as the years went by until, in 1977, they rose to £121,940,000 and £11,481,000 respectively. The factory space has increased and the work force too has become larger; this healthy situation is private enterprise at its best. The spirit and tradition of the pioneers, kept alive and energized by Lord Hives and his successors, must surely have been a major factor in the recovery of the motor company after such a devastating crash. Although the motor cars are being produced in increasing numbers, they are still of an advanced technical specification and of the highest standards of quality.

Better and more luxurious models keep coming out year after

year in increasing numbers. The quality of the cars remains superb—"the best"—so much so that it is difficult to see how they can be improved year by year, but they are. I was kindly lent a 1976 model Corniche for a day two years ago; I could not see how it could be improved! Yet when I was discussing it with an official of the company in 1978, remarking upon how good it was, he said: "That was two years ago; you should try the new ones, they are much better!" I suppose I must believe him.

The name of Rolls-Royce remains synonymous with excellence, and the magic of the name is being worthily upheld by the motor car company, now known as Rolls-Royce Motors Ltd.

It was a traumatic experience having to leave Rolls-Royce after forty-five years and in such an uncharacteristic way. Alas, there were no longer any senior directors left to say farewell; they too had gone and so I tidied up my papers and quietly departed.

To get busy again was now my aim. I wanted to stay with aviation, so that I could still be involved and associated with my many friends and colleagues in the field. So I became an aviation consultant and also started to write my first book *Rolls-Royce from the Wings*, which was published in England. It is good therapy to write a book when one is in difficulties!

As an aviation consultant, I soon found a worthy cause for my attention, albeit a far cry from sophisticated jet-engined supersonic fighters! While attending the Paris Air Show in 1973, I had learned of the need to find a suitable piston engine for agricultural aviation and crop spraying, etc. The old Pratt and Whitney air-cooled radial engines had been doing sterling service for many years, but now needed replacing. The only nine-cylinder still in production this side of the iron curtain was the British Alvis Leonides of 550/650 horsepower, which gave an improved performance at an acceptable cost. I formed a company: R. W. Harker Assoc. (Aero engines) Ltd., to market the engine in this expanding and important market. The wheel has turned full circle; now I am back where I started with piston engines and air-cooled radials at that; these were our competitors against the liquid-cooled Kestrels and Merlins thirty-five years ago!

One learns a great deal when one is self-employed; it broadens one's outlook and one has to be completely self-reliant. I think perhaps I stayed too long with "Uncle Rolls" but I did not want to leave when Sir Denning Pearson and the other senior executives I had known for so many years were still there. Leaving earlier would have been an advantage if I had been contemplating a second career.

I am really enjoying my present activities and I am sure that I would not have been so happy with the new Rolls-Royce organizations; I knew and appreciated the old one too much. I have the happiest recollections of my forty-five years with the company and consider it a privilege to have worked with and known so many fine people.

Lord Hives once remarked, "The firm started on wheels and might well finish on wheels." Could this be prophetic? It all depends on what one means by "the firm"—or does "the firm" mean the Rolls-Royce tradition? Where will this survive best? Under the aegis of the nationalized aero engine company or in the fertile soil of private enterprise with Rolls-Royce Motors?

I hope that the future may hold continuing success and prosperity, with satisfaction to the customer, pride of the workers in their product and a continuation of the spirit that inspires excellence of endeavor in future generations of engineers.

Index